A Professor's Perspective

Essays on the 45, not 46, U.S. Presidents From Washington to Biden

Essays by Dr. Herbert Barry III
Edited by John M. Baker

Many of these essays were originally shared in a column called *Herbacious Harvest* as part of *Phoenix*, a monthly newsletter of the Western Pennsylvania Mensa Society, 1986 to 1995

Copyright 2023
Published September 2023

ISBN: 979-8-9888837-0-8
Published by Ames Hill Press

Remarkable Presidential Quotes

"On matters of style, swim with the current; on matters of principle, stand like a rock." —*Thomas Jefferson (1743 - 1826)*

"The cynics may be the loudest voices—but I promise you they will accomplish the least." —*Barack Obama (1961 - Present)*

"When angry, count to 10 before you speak. If very angry, a hundred." —*Thomas Jefferson (1743 - 1826)*

"Be patient and calm; no one can catch a fish with anger." —*Herbert Hoover (1874 – 1964)*

"It is easier to do a job right than to explain why you didn't." —*Martin Van Buren (1782 - 1862)*

"The only thing we have to fear is fear itself." —*Franklin D. Roosevelt (1882 - 1945)*

"Motivation is the art of getting people to do what you want them to do because they want to do it."
—*Dwight D. Eisenhower (1890 - 1969)*

"Every expert was once a beginner." —*Rutherford B. Hayes (1822 - 1893)*

"Nobody cares how much you know until they know how much you care." —*Theodore Roosevelt (1858 - 1919)*

Table of Contents

Presidential Parallels

Introduction

John M. Baker
Nephew of Dr. Herbert Barry III
June 2023

Across the vast landscapes of notable people available to study, there is good reason to choose the ones who became President of the United States. They come from a shared American culture. To garner attention, they develop larger-than-life personalities. As Presidents, they become intricately intertwined and often represent the events of their time.

These leaders are shaped by many things – their families, their parties, and the politics of the moment. We have an impression of them as soon as we hear their names. When we learn something we didn't know, the insight illuminates much more than the person; it informs the time. As a window on history, Presidents provide an incredible view.

With great pride and admiration, I introduce to you "A Professor's Perspective: Essays on the 45, not 46, U.S. Presidents From Washington to Biden," authored by my uncle, Dr. Herbert Barry III. A Professor Emeritus at the University of Pittsburgh, Uncle Herb has always been fascinated by the U.S. Presidents and has always put his keen academic mind to writing about them.

From before the age of ten, he has seen them as a point of interest and object of study.

He developed the tools to truly evaluate them by studying Psychology. Like his father, he received his B.A. from Harvard University. In 1957, he received his M.A. and Ph.D. in Experimental Psychology from Yale University.

The Professor's Perspective is well-formed. Not everyone gets to be President, and if anyone can uncover a statistical relationship for why it happens, it is Uncle Herb. Even now, in his 93rd year, he has the curiosity of a ten-year-old and the desire to publish of a newly appointed assistant professor.

His focus is on the person that becomes President. This is why he insists Grover Cleveland was only one President despite having two non-consecutive terms. While many count him twice as President number 22 and 24, Uncle Herb is certain he was only one man and should be counted as one President. He was one person with one set of circumstances and one set of influences, even if this means renumbering all of the Presidents that followed making President Biden number 45.

The roots of this collection lie in the Western Pennsylvania Mensa newsletter called Phoenix, where Uncle Herb published a monthly column under the title "Herbaceous Harvest."

During this time, my cousins, siblings, and I would routinely receive a stack of photocopied essays, typically stuffed alongside birthday cards or Christmas letters. Each carried the Phoenix letterhead and 350-450 words examining one or multiple Presidents.

Between the stacks of papers in Uncle Herb's spare room and the sheets we collected from our files, this project started with nearly 30 essays on individual Presidents and 10 columns highlighting interesting connections between them. Intent on publishing at least one article on each President, Uncle Herb has filled in the gaps either through interviews or emails over the last 18 months.

To bring more to the history, we have included images from the time of each President.

As a boy Uncle Herb loved cartoons, and, just last year, he gave us a couple of collections taken from Boston papers during World War II. These scrapbooks were the inspiration to include cartoons, images, and magazine covers from the period of each President and the decision to make this a coffee table book.

As a professor of psychology, Uncle Herb brings a unique perspective to his analysis of the Presidents. His love for statistics and the study of names, birth orders, and parental relationships provide insights not typically found in personality-driven political summaries.

In collaboration with Uncle Herb, I have had the privilege of editing the more recent articles. It has been fascinating to work through the gaps. It has been even more incredible to see how, when the conversation turns to a President we have covered, Uncle Herb brings up the same insight he wrote 30 years ago as if it were yesterday.

"A Professor's Perspective: Essays on the 45, not 46, U.S. Presidents from Washington to Biden" pays homage to Uncle Herb's lifelong devotion to history and psychology and serves as a valuable resource for anyone seeking to delve into the legacies of our nation's leaders.

Foreword: Creating Child Citizenship

November 1991
Dr. Herbert Barry III

Each November, citizens 18 years and older are entitled to vote for or against our governmental leaders. Preparation for this act of citizenship begins in childhood, many years before eligibility to vote. It will be beneficial for our society if children look forward to voting as eagerly as many of them look forward to driving a car or buying alcoholic beverages.

Political awareness begins earlier than most adults realize. My earliest conscious memory about President Roosevelt was a few days after my tenth birthday, listening over the radio to a speech he gave at the University of Virginia. I remember the date because of a statement near the beginning of the speech, "On this tenth day of June, nineteen hundred and forty, the hand that held the dagger has struck it into the back of its neighbor." This referred to Mussolini's declaration of war on France at the time Hitler's armies had almost completed their destruction of the French armies.

I was undoubtedly aware much earlier of the President of the United States and of national and international news. My parents were very interested in these topics, and they recognized the menace of Hitler long before the beginning of World War II in 1939.

Within two months after Roosevelt's speech on June 10, 1940, I listened with great interest over the radio to the Republican and Democratic conventions. The Republican convention remains a vivid memory. Wendell L. Willkie won on the sixth ballot in a close contest with Thomas E. Dewey and Robert A. Taft. My parents were thrilled by Willkie's victory because he, like them, rejected the isolationism that characterized many of the Republican leaders. My parents had voted for Roosevelt in 1932 and 1936, but they voted for Willkie in 1940, disapproving of a third term for a President and regarding Willkie as an attractive alternative.

I was an ardent advocate of Willkie at the time of the Presidential election in November 1940, concurring with the decision of my parents rather than developing my views independently. An influence on me, however, was that in contrast to the Republican convention, the Democratic convention nominated Roosevelt on the first ballot, with a small minority of the votes for other candidates. I felt disposed to prefer the candidate who was not the incumbent and who had won a close, exciting contest. A contributor to this sentiment may have been Roosevelt's speech on June 10, 1940, which included eloquent praise of individual freedom and of the ability of the American people to choose their leaders.

Parents and other adults can create child citizenship by communicating political knowledge and concerns to children. Early development of political awareness builds a strong foundation for constructive and effective political participation in adulthood.

World War II undoubtedly contributed to the development of my political awareness. I have vivid memories of the German and Russian conquest of Poland in September 1939. The recent events in the Persian Gulf and Eastern Europe undoubtedly have had an equivalent impact on many contemporary children.

My personal memories indicate one child's development of political sentiments. Other children have other experiences, but those we remember in adulthood are only fragments of our political awareness. It begins much earlier than ten years of age. All of it contributes to our interest and constructive activity when we become voters and communicate our political convictions to our own children and to other people.

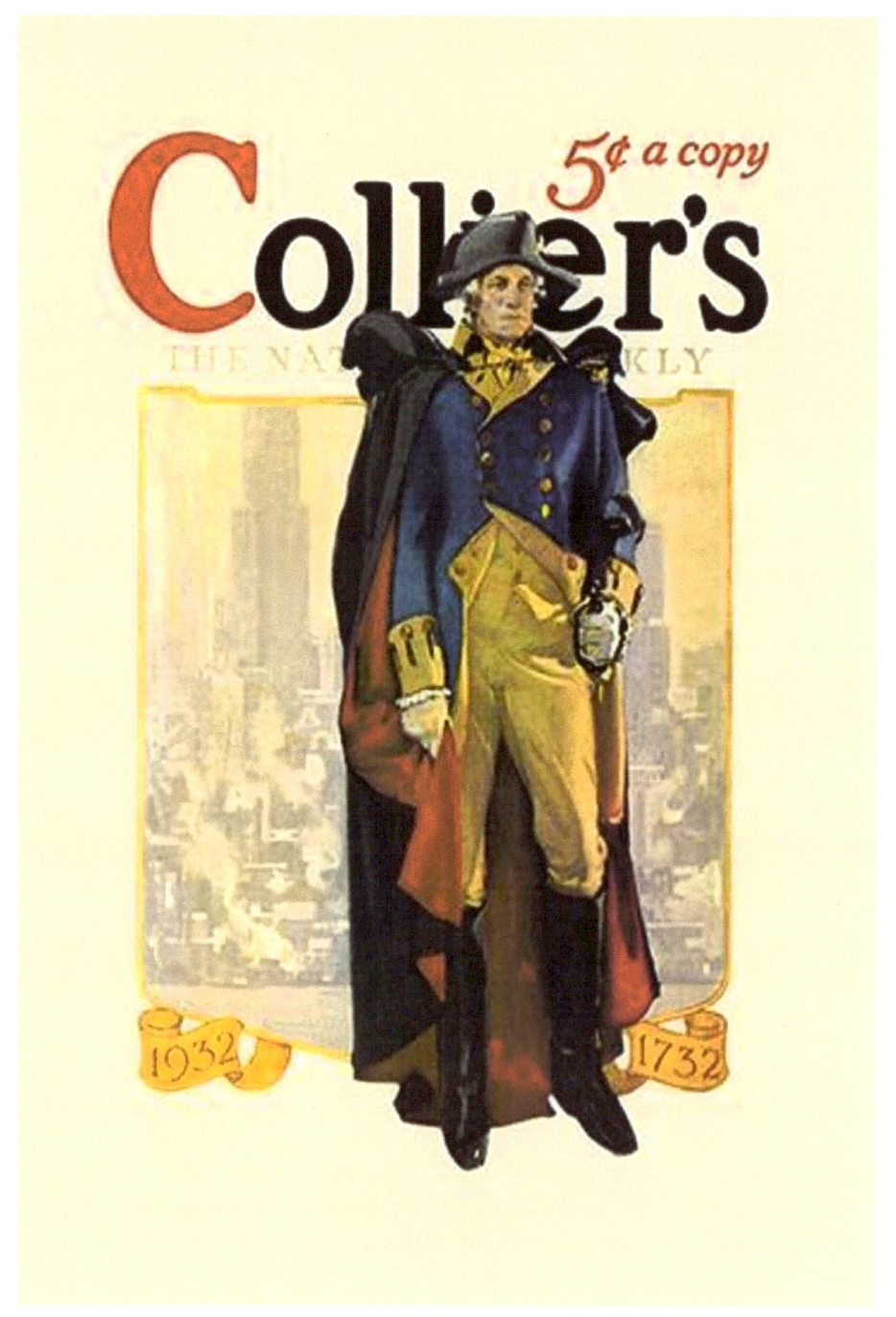

George Washington

Getting What You Really Want

February 1986

I remember vividly a wise statement by a good friend, "People usually get what they really want." This summarizes the lives of most people, and it applies especially well to George Washington.

Most Americans regard him as the revered father of our country and also as a remote character. Both perceptions fulfill his desires.

The reality that we usually get what we really want is obscured by pairs of opposing desires, such as construction and destruction, excitement and tranquility. Generally, one of the contradictory desires prevails in accordance with what we really want. The conflict between Washington's contradictory desires was unusually severe but blessed with extraordinarily favorable outcomes.

One pair of contradictory desires centered on Washington's self-control. He was impetuous and passionate but acquired formidable rationality and self-renunciation. He really wanted to become the needed leader, quelling the ambitions of others by suppressing his own desires for power and glory. His effectiveness in getting what he really wanted is indicated by the continuing survival of our free and democratic country,

Another pair of contradictory desires centered on Washington's privacy. He was gregarious and extraordinarily charming, but he really wanted to conceal his inner feelings. His detailed diary and voluminous correspondence give much information about his experiences and deeds but very little about his sentiments. His reticence contributed to his success in dealing rationally and fairly with his enormously talented and rivalrous subordinates.

A good biography is "Washington; the Indispensable Man" by James Thomas Flexner (New York: Signet Book, paperback, 1984). It is based on a four-volume biography by the author (1965-1972, published by Little, Brown). Washington's pairs of contradictory desires are portrayed vividly in the four-volume account, especially in the last chapter of the last volume.

The one-volume abridgment, which has a much larger circulation, is mostly reduced to a chronicle of his experiences and actions. This is another way in which Washington got what he really wanted. Similarly, the national holiday celebrating his birthday in February is sometimes designated as President's Day. He deserves, even if it is not what he really wanted, the recognition expressed by his name as the title of this essay.

A New DISPLAY of the UNITED STATES

John Adams

The First President Adams

October 1986

Six Presidents of the United States were born in October, more than in any other month. These were John Adams, Hayes, Arthur, Theodore Roosevelt, Eisenhower, and Carter.

John Adams, born on 30 October 1735, was the first of these six Presidents. He was also first in several other contexts.

He was the first of two Presidents Adams, father and son. After serving as the first Vice President of the United States, John Adams was the first President to win a partisan election (against Jefferson in 1796) and the first to be defeated for re-election (by Jefferson in 1800).

Another unique attribute of Adams was that his longevity, more than 90 years, exceeded all the other Presidents.

John Adams was highly individualistic, quarrelsome, and opinionated. He formed close but ambivalent attachments with several other leaders of the American Revolution. Most notable was his relationship with Thomas Jefferson.

The transition from friendship to hatred is an unfortunately frequent occurrence in human relationships. Adams and Jefferson were bitter rivals while Adams was President and Jefferson Vice President (1797-1801). Their complete estrangement originated during Jefferson's campaign to defeat Adams in the election of 1800.

Contrary to the usual persistence of hatred between two men, their friendship was restored. Beginning in 1812, they wrote many lengthy letters to each other (109 by Adams, 49 by Jefferson) during the remaining 14 years of their lives.

An amazing further linkage between them was their death on the same day, 4 July 1826, exactly 50 years after both of them had signed the Declaration of Independence. Their mutual death on this anniversary induced much comment at the time. It indicates strong evidence that an important anniversary can influence the date of death.

The improbability of two deaths on the same meaningful date is magnified by the addition of a third death on the same date. Therefore, impressive evidence for an important impact of that national anniversary was the death of the fifth President of the United States, James Monroe, exactly five years later, on 4 July 1831. It is possible but very improbable that random chance accounts for the deaths of three of the first five Presidents on this uniquely important anniversary for their country.

17

18

Thomas Jefferson

Inclinations Consistent with Ideals

Thomas Jefferson was born on 13 April 1743. He is rightly admired as one of the leaders of the American Revolution, author of the Declaration of Independence, spokesman for liberty, and outstanding educator, scientist, historian, and writer, with important further achievements in his eight years as President of the United States.

A highly likable personality accompanied his revolutionary doctrine. He was skillful at attracting friendship and respect from his contemporaries. He founded the Democratic Party, which still endures. A succession of loyal adherents followed him in the Presidency: James Madison for eight years and James Monroe for the next eight years. No other President has had such lasting influence.

Surprising inconsistency between his inclinations and ideals is revealed in a biography by Fawn M. Brodie, "Thomas Jefferson, An Intimate History (New York: W. W. Norton, 1974; Bantam Books paperback edition 1974). He owned slaves. After the death of his wife, he had several children whose mother, Sally Hemings, was one of his slaves. Her ancestry was predominantly white, in common with many other people who are classified as black.

Jefferson undoubtedly appreciated the advantages of a slave in place of a wife, especially because his liaison with Sally Hemings was preceded by a love affair with Mrs. Marie Cosway, the wife of an English artist. She was an untamed shrew. It is remarkable, however, that Jefferson's exploitation of slaves coexisted with his proclamation that "all men are created equal."

Jefferson's family and descendants tried to conceal his relationship with Sally Hemings, and some of his biographers have denied it. I believe that Fawn Brodie gives highly convincing evidence based on a combination of facts and inferences. The evidence is consistent with his complex character portrayed in her biography.

A close friend used to tell me, "You are very complex." When I commented that all humans are complex, she replied that I was more so than most people. I suspect that I appeared to be unusually complex only because she knew me unusually well. Those of us who regret the inconsistencies between our inclinations and ideals may feel reassured by the extreme example of Thomas Jefferson, whose character and achievements were predominantly admirable.

James Madison

Father of the Federalist Papers

James Madison was the first son of a prosperous Virginia colonist. He was the second of three Virginians who were close friends of Thomas Jefferson. No other Presidents of the United States have had these close affiliations.

James Madison has been called the father of the Constitution, although he disagreed with this title because he felt the Constitution was the work of many.

When the Constitution was being ratified by the states, he wrote 29 newspaper articles that described how the Constitution would function. These became known as the Federalist Papers, and they continue to have a significant impact on the judiciary today.

He, like Thomas Jefferson, was from Virginia, and the two had deep ties dating back to 1779 when Jefferson was Governor of Virginia, and Madison served on the Governor's Council.

When Jefferson, Madison and Monroe are taken together, they represent six terms – 24 years -- of governance by Virginia. This was a continuity not seen previously or afterward.

Often referred to as the "Virginia Dynasty," the relationship of these men holds a significant place in American history. United by their shared commitment to the ideals of the American Revolution, these three Presidents played pivotal roles in shaping the early years of the United States.

Their relationship extended beyond mere political alliances, as they formed a deep bond of friendship and intellectual camaraderie. Their correspondence reveals a constant exchange of ideas, wherein they discuss matters of governance, political philosophy, and the future of the young nation. Together, Jefferson, Madison, and Monroe laid the foundation for American democracy, leaving an indelible legacy that would shape the course of the nation for generations to come.

James Madison was inaugurated as President in 1809, although several New England states voted against him. In July 1812, he declared war against the British Empire even though several New England states opposed his decision.

HANDS OFF!

"This in reality entails no new obligation upon us, for the Monroe Doctrine means precisely such a guarantee on our part."—*President Roosevelt.*

James Monroe

Last of the Revolutionary War Presidents

James Monroe was President from 1817–1825 and was the last of the Presidents that were part of the founding fathers and the last to have fought in the Continental Army in the Revolutionary War.

James Monroe came to the presidency as one of the most qualified men ever to assume the office. His resume included service in the Revolutionary War, the Continental Congress, and the U.S. Senate. Monroe also served as governor of Virginia, filled numerous diplomatic posts, and held two cabinet appointments.

His success as a politician was the result of hard work and a steady and thoughtful manner. He was noted for his integrity, frankness, and affable personality, and he impressed those whom he met with his lack of pretension. As President, Monroe saw the country through a transition period in which it turned away from European affairs and toward U.S. domestic issues.

The President's relationship with his secretary of state, John Quincy Adams, was vital.

The two men had respect and admiration for each other, which led to a successful working rapport. In fact, Monroe had an ability to assemble great minds and then allow them the freedom to work. Scholars have long regarded his cabinet as an exceptionally strong one.

As President, Monroe occasionally suffers from comparison to the other members of the Virginia Dynasty. He was not a Renaissance man like Jefferson; his overwhelming interest and passion was politics.

Most people know about the Monroe Doctrine. It introduced the concept of U.S. territoriality and aimed to establish the United States as the dominant power in the Western Hemisphere and deter European colonialism. Subsequent Presidents often referenced and expanded upon the principles of the Monroe Doctrine to justify their actions. For example, President Theodore Roosevelt invoked the doctrine to assert U.S. interests in the construction of the Panama Canal and to justify American interventions in Latin American countries under the policy known as "Big Stick Diplomacy."

Both President Monroe and President Roosevelt were noted as having strong relationships with their mothers. A strong relationship with a mother can provide a solid foundation for developing a sense of self-worth and assertiveness, which can provide the motivation to stand up for one's rights.

Birthplaces of John Adams and John Quincy Adams, Quincy, Mass.

68214

68214

24

John Quincy Adams

A Disillusioned Federalist

John Quincy Adams was the first of three sons of his father, who was the second President of the United States.

Belonging to the prominent Adams family, he benefited from several advantages in his career and personal life. Firstly, his familial background provided him with a network of influential connections and political support. Being associated with a respected and established family name granted him a certain level of credibility and recognition within political circles. Growing up in a politically engaged household, Adams received an early exposure to political discourse and gained valuable knowledge and insights from his father's experiences as a statesman.

This upbringing likely shaped his intellectual development and prepared him for a career in public service.

John Quincy Adams left the Federalist Party around 1808 to become a member of the Democratic Party, then called the Democratic-Republican Party. Founded by Jefferson and Madison, the Democratic-Republican Party had become the dominant political force in the United States, advocating for a platform that is similar to the current Republican Party: limited government, states' rights, agrarianism, and strict interpretation of the Constitution.

Adams had been a member of the Federalist Party earlier in his political career and had even served as a U.S. Senator from Massachusetts as a Federalist. However, Adams became disillusioned with the party's policies and direction, particularly with regard to the ongoing tensions between the United States and Britain. He felt that the Federalist Party was too aligned with British interests and was not adequately representing American interests.

In 1824 there was no Federalist candidate. John Quincy Adams had the second most states and votes. Jackson had the most. According to an amendment to the Constitution, if no candidate received a majority of the states, the House of Representatives chose the next President, each state having one vote. The House gave a majority of votes to Adams.

His Presidency was cooperative and free from scandal. In 1828, Jackson defeated Adams, who in 1831 won election to the House of Representatives. He served as an antislavery spokesman in the House of Representatives until his death in 1848.

Causation of Coincidences

November 1986

We usually underestimate the frequency with which multitudinous events are clustered because of random chance rather meaningful associations. If two people share the same birthday, or encounter each other unexpectedly away from their usual habitats, they may erroneously attribute meaning to an accidental coincidence.

Many people would perceive an improbable coincidence if two of the 39 Presidents of the United States had been born on the same one of the 365 days of the year.

Contrary to this perception, the probability of 39 people each having different birthdays is 12%. This is much less than the 50% dividing line between probable and improbable. The probability is even less than 12% if some dates of birth are more probable than others, instead of equal probability of birth on any of the 365 days.

In accordance with the likelihood of coincidental birthdays, two Presidents shared the same birthday (2 November): James K. Polk (the 8th President) and Warren G. Harding (the 28th President). Immediately preceding Harding, the absence of coincidental birthdays among the 27 Presidents was more improbable than probable (37% probability).

Some readers might Iike to know how to calculate these probabilities.

The probability is 364/365, = .99726 that the second person has a birthday that differs from the first. A third person can have any of 363 birthdays different from either of the other two. The preceding probability of .99726 for two people Is a multiplied by 363/365 = .99452. Therefore, the probability that all three have different birthdays is (.99726)(.99452) = .99180. The probability of four people each having different birthdays is .99180 multiplied by 362/365 = .99178, thus (.99180)(.99178) = .98365. When this progression reaches 23 people, the probability is less than 50% that each of them continues to have a different birthday.

Although the coincidence of two Presidents having birthdays on the same date can be expected by chance, there may be a meaningful reason why the one birthday shared by two Presidents is in early November. This sometimes coincides with election day in the United States.

Harding was elected President on his 55th birthday in 1920, Polk 3 days after his 49th birthday in 1844. I believe that a birthday coinciding with election day increases the person's interest in politics and thereby the probability of choosing a career that results in becoming President. This belief is supported only weakly, by the coincidence of the births of two Presidents on 2 November.

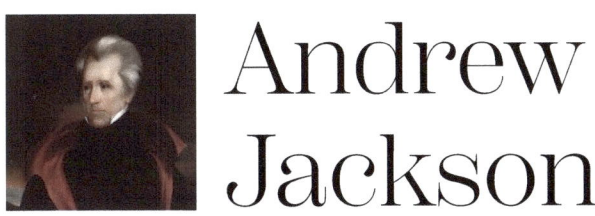

Andrew Jackson

The Ides of March

The assassination of Julius Caesar on 15 March 44 B.C. is widely remembered by the warning in Shakespeare's play, "Beware the ides of March." Andrew Jackson was born on the ides of March, 1,811 years later (in 1767 A.D.). Similarities and differences characterize these two men who are linked by the same date of 15 March.

In common with Caesar, Jackson was extraordinarily successful, both as a military leader and as a politician. Another similarity is identification with the common people against the elite establishment.

A major difference is the consequence of their careers. Caesar destroyed the Roman Republic. Jackson, who was an equivalently strong and popular leader, preserved and strengthened the constitutional government of the United States.

The difference is partly attributable to their political settings. Rome at the time of Caesar was an overextended empire, ruled by a quarrelsome oligarchy, vulnerable to overthrow by a popular army commander. The United States was a new nation with a carefully designed constitution and a heritage of wise, intelligent leadership.

The character of Andrew Jackson contributed to the beneficial outcome of his career. He submitted to the laws and traditions of the United States, which was founded during his lifetime. One of the traditions he continued was to retire after his second term as President. He supported the election in 1836 of his successor, Martin Van Buren, who had been his Vice President. Nobody since then has been elected President immediately following the completion of his term as Vice President.

Jackson's appreciation of the dangers of excessive power might have been heightened by his birth on the anniversary of Caesar's assassination. If so, the United States benefited from the coincidence of these two events on 15 March.

A further possibility is that Jackson's attitudes toward his country reproduced feelings of identification without rivalry toward his father, Andrew. The identification may have been intensified by sharing the same name. The absence of rivalry is attributable to the death of Andrew, the father, a few days before the birth of Andrew, his third son.

An 1837 lithograph published by H. R. Robinson, N.Y.

30

Martin Van Buren

Martin Van Buren, the eighth President of the United States, had a notable political career and faced significant challenges during his presidency.

Born into a Dutch heritage, Van Buren shared this ancestry with future Presidents Theodore Roosevelt and Franklin D. Roosevelt. He was also one of the few vice Presidents who went on to become President, along with George H.W. Bush. Like Bush and others, Van Buren was defeated for re-election.

Van Buren's presidency coincided with a major financial collapse known as the Panic of 1837. This economic crisis began shortly after he assumed office and persisted throughout his four-year term. Unfortunately, the economic downturn significantly affected his chances of being re-elected. Prior to becoming President, Van Buren had enjoyed a successful political career in New York State.

Despite the economic challenges, Van Buren made notable contributions during his presidency. He established Texas as an independent nation rather than a slave state and continued Andrew Jackson's policy of relocating Indian tribes from Florida to western territories. Van Buren also successfully resolved a border dispute between Maine and the Canadian province of New Brunswick. Additionally, he implemented the Independent Treasury Bill, which allowed the country's money to be deposited into its own banks rather than privately owned banks.

Van Buren developed a reputation for his ability to turn his name into a political slogan.

He expressed both pride in being elected President as Martin Van Buren and the disappointment associated with the economic collapse by referring to his presidency as "Martin Van Ruin." This phrase became part of the historical narrative surrounding his time in office.

Posthumous Paternal Power

August 1994

The father is an important influence on the personality development of his children. Even a child born after the father's death is affected by family accounts about him and is likely to identify with an idealized paternal model.

Three Presidents of the United States were born after their fathers died. I believe this country and all humanity have benefitted from the posthumous power of their fathers.

Andrew Jackson, President 1829-37, was born less than one week after his father, Andrew Jackson, died by straining himself lifting a log. Rutherford Birchard Hayes, President 1877-81, was born less than three months after his father, Rutherford Hayes, died of fever. President William Jefferson Clinton was born on 19 August 1946. More than two months earlier, his father, William Jefferson Blythe, III, had died in a single-car accident while driving home.

Tragic events can have beneficial effects, in accordance with the proverbs, "Every cloud has a silver lining," and "It's an ill wind that blows no good."

The boy, given his father's first name, was the focus of his mother's love and ambitions. He became closely bonded with her, developed social skills, and was eager to fulfill her ambitions. He did not need to submit to or compete with a powerful, punitive father. Instead, he identified with an idealized paternal model, thereby becoming both assertive and conscientious.

A boy who responds in these ways to growing up without a father has an increased probability of choosing a political career and being successful. An indication of this increased probability is that the three Presidents born after the death of their fathers constitute 7% of the 41 Presidents. Less than 1% of the total population were born after the death of their fathers.

In comparison with the other Presidents of the United States, I believe that Jackson, Hayes, and Clinton showed unusually strong expressions of three characteristics. These are interest in public service, courage, and social affiliations.

All three of these Presidents were career politicians who were highly successful, beginning in early adulthood. Their political careers expressed their willingness to compete and their desire to serve the public.

All three were unusually courageous. Jackson and Hayes were army generals known for outstanding bravery. Clinton advocated racial integration, support of President Kennedy, and opposition to the Vietnam war. These convictions were contrary to the sentiments of most of his neighbors in Arkansas.

All three showed outstanding social skills. They were strongly liked and admired by people who knew them, including their wives.

The three Presidents born after the death of their fathers differed greatly in appearance, personality, and type of achievements. I believe their differences indicate different responses to the same experience of growing up with an idealized paternal model and a mother who was a widow.

Jackson had a long, lean body and face. His most conspicuous personality characteristic was highly aggressive behavior. In social situations he was outstandingly graceful, poised, and charming. His presidency was both assertive and effective. He reoriented and revitalized the Democratic party.

Hayes, who was medium in height, had a large head with a full beard and a high forehead. He was outstandingly sociable and friendly. He was also a Civil War hero, who rose from major to major general. As a Republican President, his insistence on honest government, reforms, and conciliation of the Southern states antagonized many of the Republican leaders in Congress.

Clinton, the tallest of the three, has a plump body and head. His identification with his idealized paternal model makes him a highly conscientious President. His trials as a fatherless boy probably contributed to his empathic understanding and sharing of other people's problems. This is one of the sources of his effort to make affordable health insurance available to everybody.

My essays are usually one-way communications to readers of the Phoenix. I always welcome responses from readers, and I will be especially grateful to any readers who identify famous men and women who were born after the deaths of their fathers or whose mothers died giving birth to them. I want to do further research on identification with an idealized parental mode. In addition to three Presidents of the United States, I know that King Henry VII of England was born after the death of his father. Henry VII ended the War of the Roses and was the father of King Henry VIII.

William Henry Harrison

Short Survival February 1991

February, the shortest month, is the month of birth of the President of the United States whose incumbency was briefest. This was William Henry Harrison, born on 9 February 1773. He died of pneumonia on 4 April 1841, exactly one month after his inauguration as President.

W. H. Harrison has the distinction of being the first Whig President. The other Presidents born in February were Washington, who was the first President; Lincoln, who was the first Republican President; and Reagan, who was the first President with a prior career as a movie actor.

In accordance with the brevity of Harrison's presidency, the Whigs did not last long as a major party. They began in 1832 as the National Republicans, the conservative alternative to Jackson's Democratic party. Renamed Whigs in 1836, they were a fragile coalition of antislavery Northerners and slave-owning Southerners. The two principal leaders, Clay and Webster, were rivals. Henry Clay of Kentucky was the party's nominee for President in 1832 and 1844 and one of four nominees for President in 1838. Daniel Webster of Massachusetts was one of the other Whig nominees for President in 1838. The Whig party attempted to reconcile its disparate elements by the nomination and election of General W. H. Harrison In 1840. He was a Southerner who made a national reputation as a military leader in wars against American Indians. In 1848, the Whigs nominated and elected a military leader from the Mexican War, General Zachary Taylor. He also died in office. Either of these Presidents might have established a strong, stable Whig party if he had survived.

The Whig party was supplanted by the Republican party, founded in 1854, which was an antislavery party with virtually no representation in the southern states. In the 1860 Presidential election, the Republican nominee and the winner was Abraham Lincoln, a former Whig.

The demise of the Whig party in 1856-1860 provides a warning for contemporary Democratic and Republican leaders. The traditional political system in the United States offers voters a choice between the two major parties.

Both parties need to attract the maximum possible support, and the members need to tolerate diverse opinions within the party. Both parties are highly susceptible to being shattered by the conflict between factions that become more antagonistic toward each other than toward the rival party. This happened to the Whigs in the Presidential elections of 1836 and 1856.

If one major party becomes split, the rival party becomes dominant. Control of the government by a single party removes our most effective protection against authoritarian rule.

If both parties split into antagonistic factions, voters will be faced with a confusing and divisive competition among multiple minority parties. This happened in the Presidential election of 1860. American history might have been kinder and gentler if the Whigs had become established as a stable party combining Northern and Southern conservatives. This might have prevented the Civil War. I believe that without this bloody conflict, the Whig and Democratic parties both would have developed a consensus in favor of the peaceful abolition of slavery within a few years after 1860.

Progress toward equal status and equal opportunities for all human beings would be more advanced now in the United States if slavery and white supremacy had been abolished by peaceful political actions. The Civil War, more than a century ago, continues to leave a residue of bitterness and of conflict between North and South, between whites and blacks.

John Tyler

Entered according to act of Congress in the year 1841 T. F. Adams, in the Eastern District of Penn.

C.A. Du Bouchet, Impr.

T. F. Adams Lith. No 46 south fourth St. Phil.

36

John Tyler

The President Who Renounced His Party

March 1995

The Democratic and Republican parties both represent a broad spectrum of sentiments. Most members agree with some but not all of their party's policies. John Tyler is an unusual example of a member who renounced his party while he was President of the United States, 1841-45.

Tyler was born on 29 March 1790. He was tall and thin, with a high, broad forehead and a narrow chin so that his face looked triangular. The center of his face was dominated by a long, thin nose.

Tyler had previously shifted party allegiance. He was a Virginian slave owner whose support of the right of states to secede caused him to renounce Andrew Jackson's Democratic party. The Whig national convention, in Harrisburg, Pennsylvania, in 1839, nominated him for vice President in the election of 1840 to obtain southern support for the party. The Whig nominee for President, William Henry Harrison of Indiana, defeated the Democratic incumbent, Martin Van Buren of New York.

President Harrison died of pneumonia on 4 April 1841, one month after his inauguration. A few months afterward, President Tyler vetoed a bill supported by the Whig majority in Congress. The Whigs angrily repudiated him. The Democrats upheld his veto but refused to accept him as their leader. Tyler thereafter was a President without a party. He was unable to govern effectively.

Many people initially regarded Tyler as Acting President on the basis of the Constitution's specification that he was the recipient of the powers and duties of the presidency. Tyler insisted that he was the recipient of the full presidency. He returned unopened all letters addressed to him as Acting President. He thereby established a precedent that benefitted the eight subsequent Presidents who attained that office due to the death or resignation of the prior President.

In February 1861, Tyler was President of a conference that tried unsuccessfully to prevent the Civil War. In November 1861, he was elected to the Confederate House of Representatives. He died on 18 January 1862, shortly before he was scheduled to begin serving in that position.

In contrast to Tyler's political career, his family life appears to have been happy and harmonious. He fathered eight children with his first wife, who died in 1842, and seven children with his second wife, whom he married in 1844.

A possible future event is the renunciation of the party by the next Republican President, whether he or she is elected in 1996, 2000, or a later year. The Republican party contains several factions with single, extreme agendas, such as libertarians who oppose human services by governments, rich businessmen who demand special favors, and Christian zealots who wish to impose their beliefs on everybody. The Republican party might be captured by one of these factions, or the party might repudiate the President's faction.

Variations in Paternal Affiliation

October 1994

My essay in the August 1994 issue of the Phoenix. "Posthumous Paternal Power," discussed three Presidents of the United States who were born after the death of the father. I believe that the admirable characters and careers of these three Presidents are encouraging evidence of the ability of humans to overcome the disadvantage of growing up fatherless.

My scientific interest in paternal relationships is not limited to affiliation with a dead and presumably idealized father. I have analyzed the paternal relationships of all the Presidents of the United States. Differences among the Presidents in their childhood relationship with the father and with the brothers showed an interesting correlation with differences in their political careers. I reported this in an article "Birth order and paternal namesake as predictors of affiliation with predecessor by Presidents of the United States." It was published in Political Psychology, 1979, volume 1, number 2, pp. 61-66.

Presidents who were the first son and were given the father's first name usually were members of the same political party as the preceding President. These attributes characterized John Adams, Madison, John Quincy Adams, Buchanan, Theodore Roosevelt, Coolidge, and Ford. Carter was the only President with these childhood experiences who was the nominee of the opposing party.

Presidents who were not the first son and who had a brother given the father's first name were usually not members of the same political party as the preceding President. These attributes characterized Washington, the first President, and also William Henry Harrison, Pierce, Cleveland, Benjamin Harrison, Franklin D. Roosevelt, Kennedy, and Nixon. Taft was the only President with these childhood experiences who was politically affiliated with his predecessor.

I interpreted these finding as evidence that a first son who is given the father's first name identifies strongly with his father and with subsequent authority figures. He is then far more likely to succeed in politics by affiliating with the party in power. A later son with a brother who is given the father's name feels more rivalry toward his father and subsequent authority figures. He is therefore more likely to succeed in politics by defeating the candidate of the party in power.

My study of Presidents of the United States investigated a limited set of variables in a specialized sample. Paternal relationships are complex. Some children are deprived of a paternal role model. Others are oppressed by excessive paternal attention. The contrasting experiences can have both advantages and drawbacks.

JAMES K. POLK.

THE PEOPLE'S CANDIDATE

FOR THE

ELEVENTH PRESIDENCY

OF THE

UNITED STATES

of America.

"The question is in fact, whether we shall have the Republic without the Bank, or the Bank without the Republic"

Polk's Speech.

Approved by the Louisiana

Committee

James K. Polk

The Setter of Boundaries

James K. Polk, the 11th President of the United States, had notable family ties as a descendant of the famous Baptist preacher John Knox.

While his maternal grandfather was not primarily focused on religion, the ancestral connection influenced Polk's background. Prior to his presidency, Polk served as Speaker of the House of Representatives, though he was not initially seen as a probable candidate for the presidency. Nevertheless, his close friendship with Andrew Jackson earned him the nickname "Young Hickory."

In 1844, Polk was nominated for President and won the election with the support of the Democratic Party, despite the prevailing belief that Henry Clay of the Whig Party from Kentucky had a stronger chance of winning.

The election was close and turned on the controversial issues of slavery because both proposed the annexation of the Republic of Texas. Neither candidate was an abolitionist. Henry Clay maintained a "moderate" stance on slavery: He saw the institution as immoral, a bane on American society, but insisted that it was so entrenched in Southern culture that calls for abolition were extreme, impractical and a threat to the integrity of the Union. James Polk believed that the federal government did not have the authority to limit the expansion of slavery into western territories. As a young man, Polk had witnessed the benefits enslaved labor brought to landowners in the western territories.

Polk served only one term. His presidency was followed by his untimely death less than a month after leaving office, raising speculation about the toll the presidency takes on a person's health. It is worth noting that Jimmy Carter, another one-term President, may surpass the longevity record by reaching the age of 100.

One of Polk's significant achievements was his decision to go to war with Mexico in 1845. His intention was to address the southern border of Texas and also acquire territories in New Mexico and California. These aspirations came to fruition in 1848 when the Treaty of Guadalupe Hidalgo resulted in the United States gaining sole control over New Mexico and California.

Polk's administration also had a lasting impact on the northern border of the United States. Despite pressure from some residents demanding the border at 54 degrees 40, Polk successfully set the northern border at its present location. This decision remains the current border configuration.

Polk retired from the presidency in 1849, leaving behind a legacy that includes territorial expansion and boundary determinations.

CONGRESSIONAL SCALES,
A TRUE BALANCE.

Zachary Taylor

Presidency of an Army Commander

November 1994

Following the Gulf War of 1991, General Colin Powell and General Norman Schwarzkopf have both been urged by many people to become candidates for President of the United States. Previous army commanders who became President without political positions prior to their military fame were Zachary Taylor, Ulysses S. Grant, and Dwight D. Eisenhower.

An interesting fact is that the eight-year presidencies of Grant and Eisenhower were remarkably free from major warfare. Their martial backgrounds did not transfer to their subsequent political leadership. It is reassuring that the military heroes elected President chose peaceful policies rather than warfare.

Zachary Taylor, born on 24 November 1784, had a high, somewhat slanted forehead, partly covered by shaggy hair, and an oval rather than round face. Other features of his face were a long nose, deeply lined cheeks, and a strong chin. He was President from 4 March 1849 until his death on 9 July 1850 from a gastrointestinal illness that began five days earlier, on Independence Day. His Presidential service of one year and three months is the third shortest thus far. The Presidents with briefer service are William Henry Harrison, one month in 1841 before he died of pneumonia, and James A. Garfield, six months in 1881 before he died of injuries from an assassin's bullet.

Taylor commanded an army that won crucial victories against larger armies in the Mexican-American war. Shortly afterward, he was the last President nominated by the Whig party, which was replaced by the Republican party.

President Taylor died at a time when Congress was about to pass the Compromise of 1850. This excluded slavery from the territory that became the state of California but contained concessions for Southern slave owners, designed to prevent secession that was threatened by Texas and other Southern states. Slavery would be permitted in southwestern territories, such as New Mexico. A component of the compromise was the Fugitive Slave Law, which helped owners to recover slaves who had escaped to a different state.

Taylor was a southern slave owner, born in Virginia and a resident of Louisiana when elected President. He was opposed to the abolition of slavery in the states where it existed, but he was also opposed to the extension of slavery to the territories that were future states. He intended to veto the compromise.

The Vice President, Millard Fillmore, supported the compromise. Shortly after Fillmore became President, he signed the Compromise of 1850.

It is interesting to speculate what would have happened if Taylor had lived to veto the Compromise. He declared that secession was illegal and should be counteracted by federal military force. If southern states had seceded, the Civil War might have begun in 1850 or 1851 instead of 1861. The secession would probably have been defeated more rapidly because of President Taylor's military ability and the fewer states that would have seceded during the presidency of a southern Whig slave owner who was also a military hero.

One of the major unappreciated tragedies of American history might be the death of President Taylor. I believe that he would have prevented or defeated secession. His successors soon afterward would have abolished slavery without the massive and prolonged bloodshed of the Civil War, 1861-65. The bitter feelings engendered by that great conflict still persist more than a hundred years afterward.

RECEPTION OF PRESIDENT FILLMORE AT THE BOSTON AND ROXBURY LINES BY THE MUNICIPAL AUTHORITIES.

THE RIGHT MAN FOR THE RIGHT PLACE.

Millard Fillmore

The Last Whig President

January 1995

Millard Fillmore, born on 7 January 1800, is probably the least-known President of the United States. Among nine unelected Presidents who were Vice President when their predecessor died or resigned, the duration of his presidency was the second shortest, from 10 July 1850 to 3 March 1853. The only shorter duration of an unelected presidency was Gerald R. Ford's, from 9 August 1974 to 20 January 1977.

Fillmore has the unenviable distinction of being the last of four Whig Presidents. The Whigs were the conservative, business-oriented rival of the Democrats. A Whig nominee was one of the two principal candidates for President in five successive elections – 1836, 1840, 1844, 1848 and 1852. Fillmore was chosen as the Whig vice-Presidential nominee in 1848 because he was a politician from the northern state of New York. These attributes were attractive to northern Whigs. The Presidential nominee, Zachary Taylor, was a Southern military hero and slave owner.

Fillmore became President because of the death of Taylor. Soon afterward, Congress passed the Compromise of 1850, which included important concessions to the southern slave owners. Fillmore signed the compromise because it averted the secession by some of the southern states. I believe this act was the fatal mistake that destroyed the Whig Party. The majority of northern Whigs, including Abraham Lincoln, became alienated from Fillmore and the Whig Party. In spite of Fillmore's otherwise good record as President, he was unable to win his party's nomination as its Presidential candidate in 1852.

The loss of support from northern Whigs resulted in the election of the Democratic nominee in 1852, Franklin Pierce of New Hampshire, and also in 1856, James Buchanan of Pennsylvania. Most of the northern Whigs, including Lincoln, joined the new anti-slavery Republican party. Its first national convention was in Pittsburgh, Pennsylvania, on 22 February 1856.

In 1856 Fillmore accepted the Presidential nomination of the American "Know-Nothing" party, although he did not agree with its doctrines of opposition to Roman Catholicism in the United States and barriers against citizenship of recent immigrants. The remnants of the Whig party supported him. The Republican nominee, John C. Freemont, attracted more votes than he did. The popular vote for Buchanan was much less than the combined votes for Freemont and Fillmore.

Fillmore's wife died less than a month after the end of his presidency. Five years later, he married a wealthy widow and became a civic leader of Buffalo, New York. He supported the Union cause in the Civil War. He died on 8 March 1874, twenty-one years and five days after the end of his presidency.

If Fillmore had vetoed the Compromise of 1850 in accordance with the intention of his predecessor, I believe that he would have been reelected. The Whig Party would have survived and, before long, forced the abolition of slavery. The secession of southern states would have been averted or defeated more quickly with less bloodshed. Many Southerners were Whigs in 1850-56, but very few Southerners were Republicans in 1860-61.

The demise of the Whig party is a useful warning for the contemporary Democratic and Republican parties. They might lose the support of most of their members if their leaders make President Fillmore's mistake of yielding to the demands of minority components. The Democrats should not become the agents for racial or ideological minorities. The Republicans should not try to impose the agenda of rich people or religious fanatics.

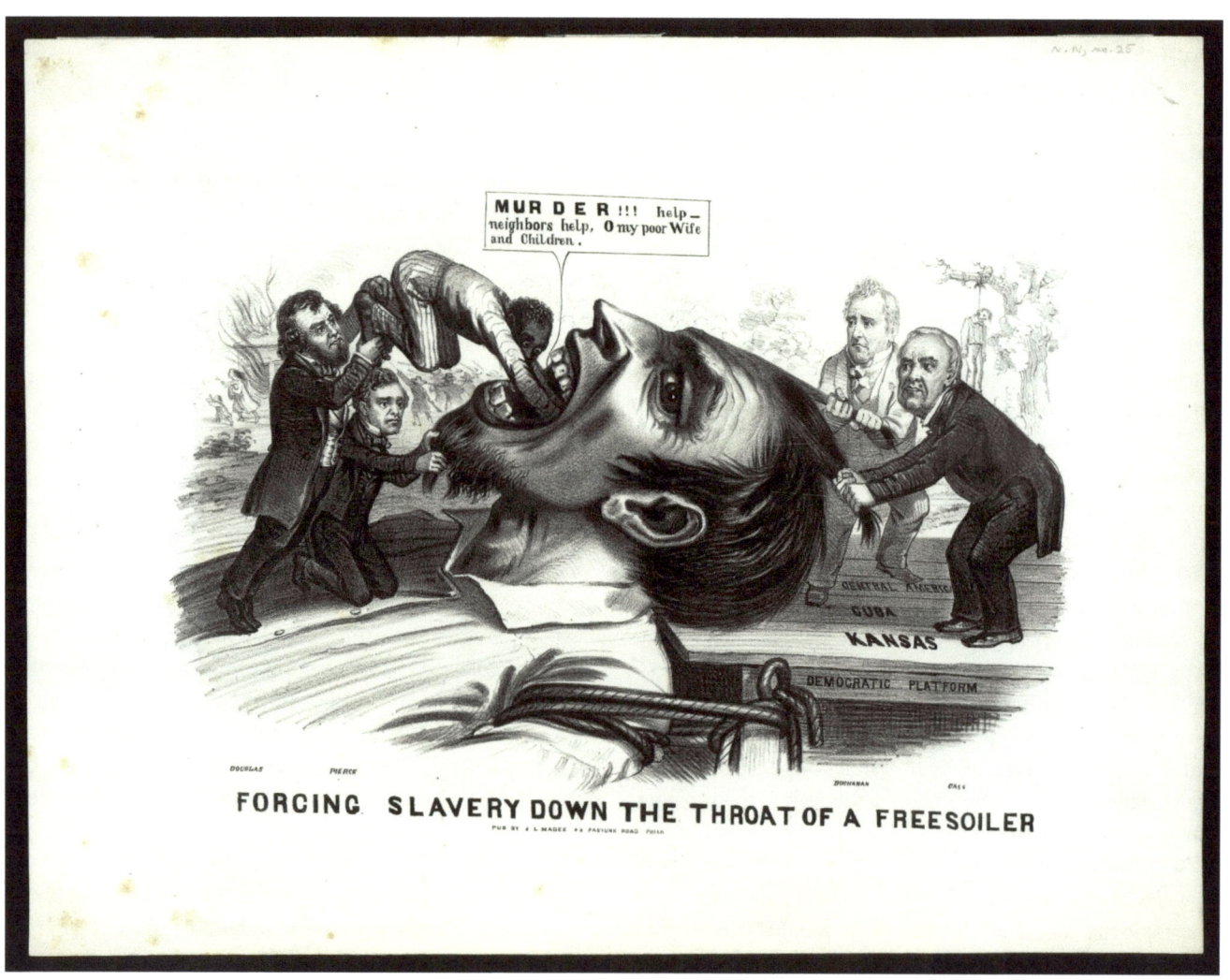

FORCING SLAVERY DOWN THE THROAT OF A FREESOILER

Franklin Pierce

Personable President Pierce

A distinguished, handsome appearance was the most conspicuous asset of Franklin Pierce, born on 23 November 1804. At the beginning of his single term as President of the United States, 1853-57, his age of 48 years was younger than all of his 13 predecessors.

Pierce was genial, kind, and ethical in his social relations. These characteristics helped him to achieve various commendable successes as President. His accomplishments did not result in a subsequent favorable reputation because historians admire Presidents who are assertive, intellectual, and reelected.

The Southern Democratic party leaders were slave owners determined to preserve and extend their "peculiar institution" of slavery. Pierce was a loyal Democrat who disapproved of slavery but, as President, antagonized many northern Democrats with his concessions to the southern Democrats. James Buchanan, a Pennsylvania Democrat who defeated Pierce for the Presidential nomination in 1856, continued the same policy as President

1857-61. Pierce and Buchanan failed to prevent the secession of the Southern states but helped the Democratic party to remain dominant in the South and to survive in the North before, during, and after the Civil War.

The Democratic party nominated for President a consecutive series of 17 northerners, of whom Lewis Cass of Michigan in 1848 was the first, Pierce of New Hampshire in 1852 the second, and Franklin D. Roosevelt of New York in 1932, 1936, 1940, and 1944 the last. Only five of them were elected President: Pierce, Buchanan, Cleveland, Wilson, and Roosevelt.

Pierce, who died of liver cirrhosis on 8 October 1869, has the unenviable distinction of being the first alcoholic President of the United States. Grant was the second and, thus far, last. The status and responsibilities of the presidency apparently helped Pierce and Grant to resist their excessive drinking because they were generally sober, conscientious, and rational in performing their Presidential duties.

LITTLE BO-PEEP AND HER FOOLISH SHEEP.

"*Little Bo-peep, she lost her sheep,*   *Let 'em alone, and they'll all come home,*
And didn't know where to find 'em;   *With their tails hanging down behind 'em.*"

# James Buchanan

Pennsylvanian President

James Buchanan was born on 23 April 1791. He is the only President of the United States thus far to represent Pennsylvania; he is also the only President born in this state (in Cove Gap).

Buchanan had a distinguished career in government, including service as the Minister to Russia for his predecessor, Franklin Pierce. Soon afterward, Buchanan defeated Pierce in a close contest for their party's nomination for President in 1856. Buchanan, therefore, succeeded, whereas corresponding contests for the party's nomination against the incumbent President were lost by Reagan against Ford in 1976 and by Ted Kennedy against Carter in 1980.

Most people who are aware of Buchanan associate him less closely with his predecessor than with his successor, Lincoln, who was one of the greatest Presidents. Buchanan appears to have been one of the least successful. At the end of his single term as President, the southern states were seceding, and he was not a candidate for a second term.

Buchanan and Lincoln were similar and both successful in some respects. Preservation of the union was their main purpose. Buchanan was a northern Democrat whose policy was to conciliate the southern slave owners, most of whom were also Democrats.

I believe that Buchanan's policy contributed to the preservation of the union by postponing the succession of the southern states. The populations of the northern states became progressively more numerous and prosperous in relation to the southern states. The Confederacy was defeated with great difficulty and hazards, 1861-1865. If secession had occurred several years earlier, I believe it would have prevailed, with detrimental effects for all Americans.

Lincoln's policies were more similar to Buchanan's than is generally recognized. Lincoln, as a candidate for President, was a moderate Republican who wished to prevent the spread of slavery but was willing to permit its continuation. His desire was conciliation of the southern states and restoration of the union, not abolition of slavery. Buchanan, whose conciliatory policy had postponed the secession of the southern states, supported the war against the Confederate States of America and thus contributed further to the preservation of the union by his successor.

Abraham Lincoln

An Eloquent Speaker

Abraham Lincoln was first elected as the 16th President of the United States in 1860. He ran as the candidate of the Republican Party, which was a newly formed political party at the time. The dynamics of the 1860 Presidential election were highly contentious and reflected the deep divisions within the United States over the issue of slavery.

The time span between Abraham Lincoln's election and the secession of the first southern state was approximately six weeks. The secession of the remaining southern states took place over a period of several months, with the last state, Tennessee, seceding more than seven months after Lincoln's election.

Lincoln was reelected in 1864 and lived to see the victorious end of the Civil War in 1865 but was assassinated five days after General Robert E. Lee's surrender at Appomattox Court House.

His successor was Vice President Andrew Johnson. He was the only Southern senator from Tennessee to be loyal to the Union. He continued the integration of the Confederate states into the Union, although he regarded the negros as an inferior race.

I have discovered that I did no Phoenix essays on Abraham Lincoln, although I have books and articles on him. I propose instead that we include three essays by him because they demonstrate his eloquence in support of the Federal union.

First is his speech in Gettysburg, Pennsylvania, in November 1862. Second is his first inaugural address as President in 1861. Third is his first inaugural speech in 1865.

All demonstrate how he spoke in support of the Union.

The Gettysburg Address

"Fourscore and seven years ago, our fathers brought forth, on this continent, a new nation, conceived in liberty and dedicated to the proposition that all men are created equal. Now we are engaged in a great civil war, testing whether that nation, or any nation so conceived, and so dedicated, can long endure. We are met on a great battlefield of that war. We have come to dedicate a portion of that field as a final resting place for those who here gave their lives, that that nation might live. It is altogether fitting and proper that we should do this. But, in a larger sense, we cannot dedicate, we cannot consecrate—we cannot hallow—this ground. The brave men, living and dead, who struggled here, have consecrated it far above our poor power to add or detract. The world will little note, nor long remember what we say here, but it can never forget what they did here. It is for us the living, rather, to be dedicated here to the unfinished work which they who fought here have thus far so nobly advanced. It is rather for us to be here dedicated to the great task remaining before us—that from these honored dead we take increased devotion to that cause for which they here gave the last full measure of devotion—that we here highly resolve that these dead shall not have died in vain—that this nation, under God, shall have a new birth of freedom, and that government of the people, by the people, for the people, shall not perish from the earth."

First Inaugural Address, 1861

Fellow-Citizens of the United States:

In compliance with a custom as old as the Government itself, I appear before you to address you briefly and to take in your presence the oath prescribed by the Constitution of the United States to be taken by the President before he enters on the execution of this office.

I do not consider it necessary at present for me to discuss those matters of administration about which there is no special anxiety or excitement.

Apprehension seems to exist among the people of the Southern States that by the accession of a Republican Administration their property and their peace and personal security are to be endangered. There has never been any reasonable cause for such apprehension. Indeed, the most ample evidence to the contrary has all the while existed and been open to their inspection. It is found in nearly all the published speeches of him who now addresses you. I do but quote from one of those speeches when I declare that--

I have no purpose, directly or indirectly, to interfere with the institution of slavery in the States where it exists. I believe I have no lawful right to do so, and I have no inclination to do so.

Those who nominated and elected me did so with full knowledge that I had made this and many similar declarations and had never recanted them; and more than this, they placed in

Second Inaugural Address, 1865

the platform for my acceptance, and as a law to themselves and to me, the clear and emphatic resolution which I now read:

Resolved, That the maintenance inviolate of the rights of the States, and especially the right of each State to order and control its own domestic institutions according to its own judgment exclusively, is essential to that balance of power on which the perfection and endurance of our political fabric depend; and we denounce the lawless invasion by armed force of the soil of any State or Territory, no matter what pretext, as among the gravest of crimes.

I now reiterate these sentiments, and in doing so I only press upon the public attention the most conclusive evidence of which the case is susceptible that the property, peace, and security of no section are to be in any wise endangered by the now incoming Administration. I add, too, that all the protection which, consistently with the Constitution and the laws, can be given will be cheerfully given to all the States when lawfully demanded, for whatever cause--as cheerfully to one section as to another.

"Fellow countrymen: at this second appearing to take the oath of the Presidential office there is less occasion for an extended address than there was at the first. Then a statement somewhat in detail of a course to be pursued seemed fitting and proper. Now, at the expiration of four years during which public declarations have been constantly called forth on every point and phase of the great contest which still absorbs the attention and engrosses the energies of the nation little that is new could be presented. The progress of our arms, upon which all else chiefly depends is as well known to the public as to myself and it is I trust reasonably satisfactory and encouraging to all. With high hope for the future no prediction in regard to it is ventured.

...

"With malice toward none with charity for all with firmness in the right as God gives us to see the right let us strive on to finish the work we are in to bind up the nation's wounds, to care for him who shall have borne the battle and for his widow and his orphan ~ to do all which may achieve and cherish a just and lasting peace among ourselves and with all nations."

PRESIDENT ANDREW JOHNSON PARDONING REBELS AT THE WHITE HOUSE.—[Sketched by Mr. Stanley Fox.]

54

Andrew Johnson

Lincoln was reelected in 1864 and lived to see the victorious end of the Civil War on April 9, 1865, but was assassinated only five days later on April 14, 1865.

His successor was Vice President Andrew Johnson. He was the only Southern senator in Tennessee to be loyal to the Union. He was a Southerner, but he continued the integration of the Confederate states into the Union.

Andrew Johnson was born on 29 December 1805 to servant parents in Raleigh, North Carolina. When Andrew was three years old, his father drowned while trying to rescue two of his employers. His mother eventually remarried, though with still little resources. At the age of 17, he moved to Greenville, Tennessee, to open up a tailor shop. Andrew Johnson held multiple local offices, including mayor. He identified as a Jacksonian Democrat (common-man ideology originating from Andrew Jackson). He got elected as a Democrat for the U.S. Senate for Tennessee.

Abraham Lincoln chose him to run as his Vice President in 1864 because he recognized the need for unity and even tried to rename the Republican Party "The Party of National Unity" but the Republicans were not in favor of it.

Lincoln's opponent was former General George McClellan, who promised if elected he would end the Civil War. Lincoln and Johnson won the election.

Before Abraham Lincoln was inaugurated, Johnson was sworn in while being very intoxicated. Lincoln commented on this and said, "I have known Andy Johnson for many years, and he is not a drinker."

When Abraham Lincoln was assassinated, Andrew Johnson became President. Since Johnson was a Democrat and most of Congress was Republican, disputes occurred between them. The House of Representatives brought impeachment proceedings against him. The House of Representatives voted in favor of impeachment. The Senate required a two-thirds majority and was one person short. The person who voted against impeachment was Edmund Ross of Kansas. Ross voted for acquittal instead of conviction. John F. Kennedy included a chapter in his book, "Profiles Encouraged," about Ross and his courageous behavior.

Andrew Johnson completed his term on 4 March 1869. He later died on 31 July 1875.

56

Ulysses S. Grant

Complex Character

Ulysses S. Grant, born on 27 April 1822, is well known as the commander of the Union armies 1864-65 and President of the United States 1869-77. His life contained a mixture of failures and successes. We human beings are all complex creatures, but Grant's character was unusually complex.

Grant had wavy brown hair. His blue eyes were deeply recessed under prominent eyebrows. The hairs of his mustache were short and curly, partly covering his thin lips. His height of five feet seven inches was shorter than all the subsequent Presidents except Benjamin Harrison.

Grant's early career was unsuccessful. He was withdrawn among strangers and in general conversation. He was an episodic alcoholic. He was forced to resign his commission as an army officer in 1854 because of recurrent drunkenness. In the next few years, he failed as a farmer and then as a real estate agent.

The Civil War was a lucky opportunity for Grant, but the opportunity by itself does not explain his ability to take advantage of it. I believe that his success is attributable to three traits: perseverance, honesty, and intellect.

Grant was extraordinarily conscientious and persistent. His motivations for alcohol intoxication probably included a craving for temporary release from his compulsive perseverance. He was consistently honest and ethical. His trustworthy character earned the devotion of his wife, children, and close friends, the loyalty of the soldiers under his command, and the decision by the Republican party leaders to choose him as the Presidential nominee in 1868 and 1872.

Intelligence was an important contributor to Grant's success. As a West Point cadet, he excelled at math. As a general, he was especially skillful in planning and coordinating campaigns and battles. As President of the United States, he understood the interrelated effects of political and governmental actions. His Presidential decisions were generally prudent and wise.

Most historians regard Grant as one of the worst Presidents of the United States. This is because of graft by some members of his administration. A contemporary politician, Chauncy M. Depew, attributed this failure to Grant's admirable character. "He was himself of such transparent honesty and truthfulness that he gauged and judged others by his own standard."

Grant finished his autobiographical memoirs less than a week before his death due to throat cancer on 23 July 1885. The same historians who evaluate his presidency as one of the worst regard his military leadership as excellent and his memoirs as the best by any former President.

Pre-Presidential
Name Changes

July 1993

Most males in our contemporary society keep the same name they were given at birth. Many boys and men have nicknames, but most of them do not change their initial given name. The first 17 Presidents of the United States likewise kept their initial given names. Among the subsequent 24 Presidents, from Grant to Clinton, eight changed their names. Modification of the personal name therefore characterized an average of one out of every three of these 24 most recent Presidents. This is conspicuously more frequent than among the total male population.

The first President who changed his name, Grant, was the first President elected after the Civil War. The pre-presidential name changes therefore are associated with the time when the President became the leader of the previously antagonistic Union and Confederate states, while the country expanded to the west coast and the federal government greatly increased its powers.

The name changes by two Presidents were probably influenced by a desire to use the mother's premarital surname. Hiram Ulysses Grant was mistakenly registered at West Point as Ulysses Simpson Grant. He retained his altered name, which included his mother's family name, Simpson. Thomas Woodrow Wilson's childhood nickname was Tommy, but he subsequently omitted his first name from his signature and other uses. Woodrow was his mother's family name.

Two Presidents, named after their fathers, modified their names due to the remarriage of their mothers. Leslie Lynch King Jr. became Gerald Rudolff Ford Jr. when he was adopted by his stepfather at the age of 3 years. The stepson subsequently changed the spelling of his middle name to Rudolf.

William Jefferson Blythe, IV at the age of 15 years changed his surname to Clinton to share the surname of his mother, stepfather and half-brother. He usually substituted the nickname Bill for his first two names, but William Jefferson Clinton was the name he stated in his oath of office as President.

Avoidance of confusion with the same first name as the father was an incentive for the name modification by three Presidents. John Calvin Coolidge began using his middle rather than first name during childhood. He was the first of these eight Presidents to be elected by women in addition to men. David Dwight Eisenhower as a boy began reversing the sequence of his first two names. James Earl Carter Jr. replaced his first two names with Jimmy for all official uses, including his oath of office as President of the United States.

The remaining President who changed his name is Stephen Grover Cleveland. He omitted his first name from his signature and other uses when he was a young man. He probably decided that Grover was a more distinctive and attractive name than Stephen.

The name change by eight Presidents is associated with a typical feminine behavior because each of their mothers and many other women changed their names when they acquired their husband's surname. I suggest that the unusual masculine behavior by the eight Presidents who modified their given names was a concomitant of unusual empathic understanding of females. This developed from a strong affiliation with their mothers and subsequently contributed to predominantly close relationships with their wives.

Rutherford Birchard Hayes

Early Retirement

October 1995

Three Presidents of the United States who completed an elected four-year term did not seek reelection. The most recent was Rutherford B. Hayes, born on 4 October 1822, President 1877-1881.

When Hayes won the Republican nomination for President in 1876, he promised not to seek a second term, lest patronage be used to secure his reelection. He believed that a President's effort to be reelected would conflict with his duty to serve the country. Accordingly, his inaugural address included the proposal for a constitutional amendment to limit the President to a single six-year term.

Hayes was a sensitive, introspective, scholarly man who developed outstanding leadership and political skills. He was a highly successful and courageous general in the Union Army in the Civil War. He subsequently became a popular politician and was governor of Ohio at the time of his election to the presidency. His kind, sociable personality counteracted the stern impression conveyed by his bushy beard and moral rectitude.

President Hayes was a reformed and also a skillful politician. His inaugural address contained the statement, "He serves his party best who serves his country best." He strengthened and united the Republican party while defying some of the party's powerful, corrupt leaders. An outstanding success by Hayes was in the Presidential election of 1880. His enthusiastic support of the Republican candidate, James A. Garfield of Ohio, resulted in the election of Garfield in a close contest against the Democratic candidate, Winfield S. Hancock of Pennsylvania. Hayes was a loyal Republican who believed that service for his party was service for his country.

An example of the political astuteness of Hayes was his decision to abolish liquor from the White House. He became a total abstainer to set a good example. Most people attributed this Presidential decision to the influence of his wife, Lucy, who advocated prohibition. She was derisively called "Lemonade Lucy." The purpose of his decision was to prevent the large number of Republican prohibitionists from joining the Prohibition Party.

The two prior elected Presidents who did not seek reelection were James K. Polk of Tennessee, President 1845-1849, and James Buchanan of Pennsylvania, President 1857-1861. Both of them, and also Hayes, expressed great relief when their single terms ended.

For readers interested in biographies of Presidents, I recommend a book published in 1995, "Rutherford B. Hayes; Warrior and President' by Ari Hoogenboom (Lawrence, Kansas: University of Kansas Press). Hayes compares favorably in character and Presidential success with most of the other Presidents, both before and after his four years of service.

James Abram Garfield

James A. Garfield, the 20th President of the United States, was born in 1831 in Ohio. Garfield was named after his father, James Garfield, who had passed away before his birth.

The interesting aspect of Garfield's name was that he rarely used his middle name. He often signed his name simply as "James A. Garfield" without explicitly stating the middle name "Abram."

Ulysses S. Grant was commonly was referred to as "Simpson" to distinguish himself from another Ulysses Grant at that time. Rutherford B. Hayes regularly used his full name, including his middle name, Birchard. Grover Cleveland, born Stephen Grover Cleveland, adopted his middle name, Grover, to distinguish himself.

Garfield's family had modest beginnings, and he grew up in a humble rural setting. During the Civil War, Garfield served as a General in the Union Army.

His military career showcased his leadership abilities and commitment to his country. However, Garfield resigned from the army to pursue a career in politics. He successfully was elected to the House of Representatives, where he became known for his eloquence and dedication to public service.

In 1880, Garfield secured the Republican nomination for the presidency, marking a significant milestone in his political journey. He faced a challenging and closely contested election against his Democratic opponent, Winfield Scott Hancock. Ultimately, Garfield emerged as the victor, winning the presidency and preparing to take office.

Just a few months into his presidency, tragedy struck. In July 1881, Garfield was assassinated by Charles J. Guiteau, a disgruntled office seeker. He was shot at a train station in Washington, D.C., and Garfield was mortally wounded. Despite receiving medical care, his condition worsened, and he passed away in September 1881, only a few months after his inauguration.

Garfield's assassination deeply impacted the nation, sparking outrage and grief across the country. His untimely death cut short what could have been a promising Presidential term. The loss of Garfield highlighted the dangers and risks associated with public service.

Chester Alan Arthur

Unexpected Success

March 2023

Chester A. Arthur's name and family background played an important role in his life and presidency.

As the son of a Baptist minister, he inherited the name "Chester" from his paternal grandfather and "Alan" from a family friend. It was his middle initial "A." that would become widely recognized during his political career, standing for "Alan" rather than a specific name. This distinctive use of his initial added to his public persona.

Arthur's birth order as the second of six children shaped his character and ambitions. Growing up in a modest household, he witnessed the hard work and dedication of his parents, William and Malvina Arthur. Their values of education, integrity, and ambition influenced his path and motivated him to strive for success.

Arthur's family connections would also come into play during his presidency. Despite being born into a family of modest means, he later married Ellen Lewis Herndon, the daughter of a wealthy Virginia family. Ellen would have brought grace and elegance to the White House as the wife of the Vice President or First Lady. Unfortunately, Ellen tragically passed away before Arthur assumed the presidency.

He served in the Union Army during the Civil War. After the Civil War, he was the Collector of Customs in New York state.

He was a Republican and was nominated for Vice President of the United States in 1880. He was elected vice President in 1881. The President-elect was James A. Garfield. He became President when James A Garfield was assassinated early in his term on 2 July 1881.

Contrary to most expectations, he became a reformer of the Civil Service. He supported the Pendleton Civil Service Reform Act, which aimed to replace the spoils system with a merit-based system for government appointments. He suffered health problems throughout and after his presidency. He suffered severe kidney ailments.

He died on 18 November 1886, more than five years after leaving office. His presidency was more admirable than what had been expected.

Grover Cleveland

Righteous Reformer

An advantage of the competition between two political parties is that the weaker party tries harder to unify its members and choose a respected, electable candidate. An example was the Democratic party in 1884.

The Republicans had won each Presidential election between 1860 and 1880. The Democrats included a fragile coalition of southern white racists, northern urban laborers, and Western populists. They cooperated to nominate for President Grover Cleveland, a righteous reformer with an impressive record as a county sheriff, mayor of Buffalo, and governor of New York. He was born on 18 March 1837, the fifth of nine children of a Presbyterian minister.

Cleveland was also the Democratic nominee in 1888 and 1892. In all three successive Presidential elections, he won less than 50% of the popular vote but won more votes than any other candidate. He won the majority of electoral votes in 1884 and 1892 but not in 1888. He is the only President who has served two nonconsecutive terms.

In 1884 the Republican nominee, James G. Blaine, had a tarnished reputation as a recipient of graft from a railroad company. Cleveland won 49% of the popular vote, Blaine 48%.

President Cleveland fulfilled his reputation as an honest executive. He also had contentious relationships with Congress, including some in his own party. He exercised the veto power more times than had all his predecessors combined. He antagonized the Democratic leaders of New York City.

In 1888 the Republicans nominated Benjamin Harrison, a Civil War general with a reputation for honesty. Harrison defeated Cleveland, although the popular vote percentages for the Democratic and Republican nominees were the same as four years earlier.

The Presidential election of 1892 was a rematch between Cleveland and Harrison. A saying at the time was that Harrison had no friends, and Cleveland had only enemies. The nominee of the People's Party, James B. Weaver, took many votes from both the Democratic and Republican nominees. Cleveland won 46% of the popular vote. Harrison 43%, Weaver 9%.

The Presidential elections of 1888 and 1892 have several resemblances to 1988 and 1992. In 1888 and 1988, a Republican was elected President. In 1892 and 1992, he was defeated by a Democrat who won less than 50% of the popular vote. All four elections were close contests in which the two major parties both nominated widely respected, politically experienced candidates.

Cleveland's last words before he died on 24 June 1908 were, "I have tried so hard to do right." His integrity was a good influence on the presidency and on the Democratic party. His deficiencies in political skill detracted from his effectiveness. I hope that President Clinton will emulate Cleveland's integrity while continuing to use the political skill that helped him to be elected governor of Arkansas several times and President of the United States in 1992.

Minority President

July 1994

Clinton was elected President of the United States in 1992 with less than 50% of the popular vote. Previous minority Presidents were John Quincy Adams (1824), Polk (1844), Taylor (1848), Buchanan (1856), Lincoln (1860), Hayes (1876), Garfield (1880), Cleveland (1884 and 1892), Benjamin Harrison (1888), Wilson (1912 and 1916), Truman (1948), Kennedy (1960), Nixon (1968), and Carter (1976).

Most of these minority Presidents, including Clinton, received more votes than any other candidate but less than a majority of the votes cast for all the candidates. Only three Presidents received fewer popular votes than a rival candidate. They are John Quincy Adams (1824), Hayes (1876) and Benjamin Harrison (1888).

When no candidate for President receives a majority of the electoral votes, the House of Representatives chooses among the three with the most electoral votes. This has happened only twice thus far. Both times, the choice was determined by a single politician who was not one of the three candidates.

In 1800, when President John Adams was a candidate for reelection, the electoral votes were 73 for Aaron Burr, 73 for Thomas Jefferson, 65 for Adams, 64 for Charles Pinckney, and 1 for John Jay. Alexander Hamilton, a supporter of Adams, persuaded some other Adams supporters to vote for Jefferson.

In 1824, John Quincy Adams, son of John Adams, won fewer popular and electoral votes than Andrew Jackson. The electoral votes were 99 for Jackson, 84 for Adams, 41 for William H. Crawford, and 37 for Henry Clay. The House of Representatives chose Adams because of support by Clay. The maneuver to prevent the election of Jackson damaged the political reputations and futures of both Adams and Clay. Jackson defeated Adams in the Presidential election of 1828.

John Quincy Adams was born on 11 July 1767. His most distinctive political characteristic is not his election as a minority President but his uniquely long and distinguished career of public service before, during, and after his presidency. He was Minister to the Netherlands 1794-97, Minister to Prussia 1797-1801, United States Senator from Massachusetts 1803-08, Minister to Russia 1809-1814, Minister to Great Britain 1815-17, and Secretary of State 1817-25.

After his Presidential term, 1825-29, Adams was a member of the United States House of Representatives from 1831 until his death on 23 February 1848, in the United States Capitol Building. He was a leader of the anti-slavery abolitionists and earned the nickname of Old Man Eloquent.

$ 100.000.000
SURPLUS LEFT
BY CLEVELAND
IN 888

BILLION- DOLLARISM ' HOLE

Benjamin Harrison

An Electoral Winner

Benjamin Harrison was elected as a Republican.

He was a grandson of the ninth President, William Henry Harrison, and great-grandson of Benjamin Harrison V, a founding father. Other Presidents that were related to Presidents included John Quincy Adams, who was John Adam's son, Franklin Delano Roosevelt, who was the fifth cousin to Theodore Roosevelt, and George W Bush, who was George HW Bush's son.

Standing only 5 feet, 6 inches tall, his opponents from the Democratic party called him "Little Ben." Republicans replied that he was big enough to wear the hat of his grandfather, "Old Tippecanoe."

He served for the Union in the Civil War as a Colonel and later achieved the rank of Brigadier General.

He defeated the incumbent, President Grover Cleveland. He won the majority of the electoral college but did not win the popular vote. Like in 2000, the presidency came down to winning one state. In 1888, Benjamin Harrison won New York, which carried enough electoral votes to be elected. He lost the popular vote by 89,293 votes.

Only one President before Harrison won the electoral college without winning the national vote, and that was Rutherford B Hayes in 1876. John Quincy Adams, in 1824, did not win the popular vote or the electoral college. The election was decided by the U.S. House of Representatives.

Since 1888, Al Gore lost to George W. Bush in 2000 by losing Florida despite having 537,000 more popular votes, and Hillary Clinton lost to Donald Trump despite having 2.9 million more votes.

The most perplexing domestic problem Harrison faced was the tariff issue. High tariff rates had created a surplus of money in the Treasury. Republican leaders in Congress, including Senator William McKinley, passed even higher tariffs as a form of protectionism. The U.S. government spending grew to over $1 billion in a single year which consumed the surplus. In 1892, Grover Cleveland was re-elected President due to the unpopularity of the high tariffs and high federal spending.

PRESIDENTIAL TRAIN.

Copyrighted by C. M. Bell, Photographer, 1887.

Grover Cleveland

Grover Cleveland holds a unique place in American history as the only President to be re-elected in 1892 after being out of office.

Born on March 18, 1837, he initially bore the name Stephen Grover Cleveland. As a child, he renounced the use of his first name and became known simply as Grover Cleveland. His father, a clergyman, instilled in him a sense of morality and integrity that would shape his political career.

During his youth, Cleveland and a group of boys were involved in a scandalous incident with a young woman. As the only bachelor among them, he assumed responsibility for the child she conceived. This incident became fodder for political attacks, with Republicans mocking him by asking, "Ma, who's my father?" to which Democrats retorted, "Gone to the White House HA HA HA." Despite the controversy, Cleveland remained resilient and focused on his political aspirations.

In 1885, Cleveland achieved a remarkable feat by winning his first Presidential election. The race was closely contested, with many Republicans crossing party lines to vote for him over Republican Senator James G. Blaine. Simultaneously, numerous Democrats, known as Mugwumps, cast their votes for Cleveland. This victory made him the 22nd President of the United States.

Cleveland's time in office was not without challenges and in 1888, he was defeated in his bid for re-election, losing to Benjamin Harrison, the grandson of President William Henry Harrison.

In 1892, Cleveland once again emerged as a contender for the presidency, engaging in another closely contested election. The key debate was over economic policies, particularly the issue of tariffs. During the election, Cleveland, a Democrat, advocated for lowering tariffs on imported goods, while his opponent, Republican President Benjamin Harrison, supported protective tariffs to benefit domestic industries. Many Americans felt lower tariffs would lower prices and increase economic growth. His victory in the election was seen as a referendum on the tariff issue and reflected a desire for a change in economic policy. Victorious, he became the only President thus far to serve two non-consecutive terms.

While many historians classify him as a President with two interrupted terms, he was only one person and one President. It is more accurate to recognize him as the 22nd President, altering the total count of Presidents. This adjustment means that President Joe Biden is correctly identified as the 45th President, not the 46th.

Throughout his tenure, Cleveland stood firm on matters of international morality, believing in the equality of nations before the law. He famously stated, "I mistake the American people if they favor the odious doctrine that there is no such thing as international morality; that there is one law for a strong nation and another for a weak one." This conviction exemplified his commitment to fairness and justice in foreign relations.

CHAMPION McKINLEY OPENS THE TARIFF BATTLE.

An unequal match between the heavy and the light weights

William McKinley

Magnifying Markets

A century ago, Democratic President Grover Cleveland 1885-89 and 1893-97 advocated lower tariffs. Lower tariffs reduce the prices of foreign products, and jobs are created in our country when exports are stimulated by the reciprocal lower tariffs of foreign countries. Republican Presidents Benjamin Harrison 1889-93 and William McKinley 1897-1901 advocated high tariffs to protect American businesses from cheap labor and products abroad.

William McKinley, born on 29 January 1843, represented a district in Ohio as a member of the U.S. House of Representatives in 1877-83 and 1885-91. He was the principal champion of high tariffs and sponsor of the exorbitantly high McKinley tariff in 1889.

McKinley indicated a change in policy less than a year after his election for a second term. He advocated reciprocal trade agreements in a speech on 5 September 1901 at the Pan-American Exposition in Buffalo. "The period of exclusiveness is past. The expansion of our trade and commerce is the pressing problem. Commercial wars are unprofitable. A policy of goodwill and friendly trade relations will prevent reprisals.

Reciprocity treaties are in harmony with the spirit of the times; measures of retaliation are not."

McKinley did not have the opportunity to act in accordance with this speech. An anarchist shot him on the next day. He died of the wound on 14 September 1901. If he had proposed a reciprocity treaty for lower tariffs, the treaty would probably have been opposed by the majority of the Republicans in Congress but supported by the majority of the Democrats.

The positions of the two parties are now reversed. Reduction of tariffs is supported by the majority of Republicans and opposed by the majority of Democrats in Congress. In 1993, 92 years after William McKinley's death, William Clinton persuaded Congress to ratify a reciprocity treaty for lower tariffs. This is the North American Free Trade Agreement (NAFTA) with Canada and Mexico. Democratic President William has done what Republican President William might have done if he had not been assassinated.

Reciprocal reduction of tariffs has the beneficial effect of extending markets over a wider territory and larger population. This extension provides buyers with a larger number and greater variety of products. Prices are lower because large quantities can be made and sold more economically. Competition among a larger number of sellers forces them to minimize their profits.

August 3 1912   HARPER & BROTHERS, N. Y.   Price 10 Cents

Theodore Roosevelt

The First President Roosevelt

Theodore Roosevelt was born on 27 October 1858. When he became vice President of the United States in 1901, at the age of 42 years old, he was the second youngest in that office. John Cabell Breckinridge, in 1857, at 36 years, was the only younger predecessor. Subsequent Vice Presidents Nixon in 1953 and Quayle in 1989 were younger than Roosevelt but older than Breckinridge.

When President McKinley died on 14 September 1901, Roosevelt, at the age of 42 years, was younger than any prior President. All his successors thus far have been older. Kennedy was 43 years old when elected in 1960.

Theodore Roosevelt was a very popular and achieving President. He was the fifth vice President to become President because of the death of the President, but in 1904 he was the first to be elected President after completing his predecessor's term. He chose his successor, William Howard Taft, and helped him to win the election of 1908.

It is an ironic reversal of fortune that Theodore Roosevelt is now less widely known than Franklin Delano Roosevelt, a distant cousin who was born in 1882. When young Franklin in 1905 married Anna Eleanor Roosevelt, the daughter of Theodore's deceased brother, President Theodore Roosevelt gave the bride away and dominated the wedding ceremony. This was consistent with a saying about Theodore Roosevelt that he wanted to be the bride at every wedding and the corpse at every funeral.

There are several correspondences between the careers of the two Presidents Roosevelt. Both were successively reformist New York state legislators, Assistant Secretary of the Navy, governor of New York, and President of the United States. After their services in the Navy department, 1897-1898 for Theodore, 1913-1920 for Franklin, the progression to the presidency was much more rapid for Theodore. He became a war hero in 1898, was elected governor of New York in the same year, was elected vice President of the United States two years later and became President less than a year afterward. Franklin, who would have replaced Theodore as the second youngest vice President if James M. Cox and he had won the election of 1920, was elected governor of New York in 1928 and President in 1932.

The first President Roosevelt was also the second Theodore Roosevelt, his father's namesake and first son. Father Theodore was the only man for whom President Theodore professed complete admiration and any submission. The son Theodore became much more impressive and famous than his diligent, dutiful, widely respected, wealthy father.

Some of the traits and actions of son Theodore indicate covert rebellion against his paternal authority figure. The son's brilliant intellect was accompanied by bellicose behavior and bombastic speech. He was highly controversial as a Republican President allied with reformers. He was addicted to physical combat, hunting large animals, and acrimonious disputes. He tried to replace Taft as the Republican nominee for President in 1912, and by competing as the nominee of the Progressive Party, he split the Republican vote, causing the election of Woodrow Wilson.

The two Presidents Roosevelt differed greatly in personality. Theodore was much more overtly assertive but a less effective politician. This difference is partly attributable to their relationships with their fathers. When son Theodore was born, father Theodore was 27 years old. The son suffered severe asthma in childhood and his father was a nurturing but powerful presence. When Franklin was born, his father, James, was 51 years old. The father was primarily a benign friend rather than a paternal authority.

FIFTEEN CENTS

TIME

The Weekly News-Magazine

MR. CHIEF JUSTICE
"Sitting on the St. Lawrence—"
(See Page 4)

VOL. III   NO. 26   JUNE 30, 1924

William Howard Taft

The Greatest President

Only one President of the United States was born in September (William Howard Taft on the 15th, in 1857). This number is unusually small. Besides June, with none, only one other month contains the birthdays of fewer than three Presidents (Truman and Kennedy in May).

A weighty criterion compensates for the deficiency in the number of Presidents born in September. Taft, who exceeded 300 pounds, was the greatest President by this objective, quantitative criterion.

There is a saying that fat men are jolly because they cannot fight and cannot run. This is a valid although incomplete explanation for Taft's cheerful disposition, which contributed to his nomination and election to the presidency in 1908.

Prior to Taft's nomination, Chauncey Depew, an elderly Senator, introduced him to an audience as "a man pregnant with hope, pregnant with faith, pregnant with charity, the next President of the United States." Taft's response indicated his wit and also his reluctance to become President. With his big belly protruding, he said, "I seem to be in a very interesting condition. If it is a boy, I will name it Hope. If it is a girl, I will name it Faith. And if it is a bag of wind, I will name it Chauncey Depew."

After his election, Taft expressed fear "that I shall be like the man who went into office with a majority and went out with unanimity." An article in the New York Times commented that Taft's "bump of political sagacity was a dent." An example was his honest statement to an important supporter, "They tell me I ought to remember you but, bless my soul, I cannot recall you at all!"

The presidency is usually the pinnacle of the incumbent's career. For Taft, it was the abyss. Nevertheless, a happy ending transforms tragedy into comedy. Taft's career can be summarized by the title of Shakespeare's comedy "All's Well That Ends Well."

In 1913 he was offered the Kent Chair of Constitutional Law at Yale. He replied jocularly that a chair would not be adequate for him, but perhaps a "sofa of law" would do. After eight years as a professor, his true ambition was fulfilled by his appointment as Chief Justice of the Supreme Court. He served well and happily from 1921 until he resigned because of illness in 1930, slightly more than a month before his death.

Contrasting Characteristics

February 1988

Complex personalities are prevalent among Presidents of the United States. Election to this position requires extraordinary ambition and achievement combined with the contrasting characteristic of a pleasing personality that elicits popularity among other politicians and the public.

More than the usual complexity characterizes Abraham Lincoln and Ronald Reagan. They have several attributes in common. Both were born in the first half of February (the 12th in 1809 for one, the 6th in 1911 for the other). One was the first Republican, the other is the most recent Republican to be elected President. Both cultivated reputations for geniality rather than brilliance in spite of their outstanding successes.

Lincoln's outstanding intellect is emphasized in an excellent biography by Stephen B. Oates "With Malice toward None; The Life of Abraham Lincoln" (New York: Harper & Row, 1977; paperback Mentor book 1978). There are many examples of his contrasting characteristics. He told funny stories but was melancholy. He advocated and planned reconciliation while conducting a brutal war. He was logical and analytical, a superb lawyer prior to his presidency, but at times he expressed belief in superstitions, signs, visions, and dreams. He was friendly and popular but concealed his inner feelings, even from his closest friends. A colleague commented "He made simplicity and candor a mask of deep feelings carefully concealed."

Ronald Reagan likewise conceals his deep feelings according to several accounts, including an informative biography by Laurence I. Barrett, "Gambling with History: Ronald Reagan in the White House" (Garden City, N.Y.: Putnam, 1983; paperback New York: Penguin book 1984). He is emotionally detached from his children and from his brother. His wife Nancy seems to be the only person he really opens up to.

Secretiveness of some people has the purpose of concealing deficiencies of character or intellect. Many Mensa members may feel special affinity for Lincoln and Reagan because their secretiveness conceals intellectual strengths rather than weaknesses.

A Wilson campaign truck offered New York City voters a convenient summary of the 1916 Democratic platform. The eight-hour-day plank refers to the president's support of a federal law for railroad workers.

Woodrow Wilson

A Democratic Progressive

Woodrow Wilson, originally named Thomas Woodrow Wilson, was known as "Tommy" during his youth. The name Woodrow came from his mother's maiden surname, Janet "Jessie" Woodrow. In his early adulthood, he decided to change his name from Thomas to Woodrow, which he would use as his first name.

Growing up, Wilson's father was a preacher who resided in the Confederate State of Georgia during the Civil War. Despite his fragile health, Wilson had a fondness for playing with toy soldiers, sparking his early interest in military affairs.

As he entered adulthood, Wilson immersed himself in the study of the United States Constitution. He enrolled in the College of New Jersey (now Princeton University), eventually becoming a professor and later serving as the university's President. It was during this time that he carefully considered an invitation to run for Governor of New Jersey, seeking the counsel of his wife and three daughters before accepting the opportunity.

After securing the Democratic nomination for governor, Wilson's successful tenure in that position propelled him to become the Democratic Party's nominee for President of the United States. His inaugural address as governor received widespread admiration, further bolstering his political standing. During his first term as governor, Wilson emerged as a successful candidate for the presidency, benefiting from a split within the Republican Party between William Howard Taft and the Progressive Party.

Despite being a Conservative Republican, my paternal grandfather, who was a senior partner in a Wall Street law firm, voted for Wilson due to the Progressive Republican Party's stance on electing Federal and State judges, an issue he strongly opposed. It highlights the influence and appeal Wilson had across party lines.

Wilson's life was the subject of various biographies, including a highly regarded one by George & George, a brother-sister duo. Similarly, a critical psychobiography of Wilson by Freud and Bullitt shed light on his character, although it faced scrutiny for its psychoanalytic terminology. Both books contained similar information and criticisms of Freud's psychoanalytic jargon, yet they were commendable in their examination of Wilson's life and presidency.

While Wilson had significant achievements, such as his progressive policies and reforms, he also made mistakes. One notable misstep was his refusal to involve Republican leaders in his plans for the League of Nations, resulting in the United States Congress rejecting membership in the league.

Warren G. Harding

Warren G. Harding, the 28th President of the United States, is often regarded as one of the least effective Presidents in American history. Despite his presidency being marred by scandal and controversy, there is one notable decision that stands out as a positive achievement: his appointment of William Howard Taft as Chief Justice of the Supreme Court.

Born on November 2, 1865, in Corsica, Ohio, Harding was the eldest of eight children.

Harding's presidency, which spanned from 1921 to 1923, faced numerous challenges and setbacks. His administration was plagued by corruption scandals, including the infamous Teapot Dome scandal, which involved the illegal leasing of federal oil reserves. These scandals tarnished his reputation and raised questions about his leadership abilities.

Despite the controversies, Harding displayed a keen eye for selecting capable individuals for key positions.

One such instance was his choice of William Howard Taft as Chief Justice of the Supreme Court. Taft, who had previously served as President from 1909 to 1913, possessed a deep understanding of the law and a reputation for judicial integrity. Harding's decision to appoint him to the highest judicial position demonstrated his recognition of Taft's legal expertise and commitment to upholding the principles of justice.

Taft's tenure as Chief Justice marked a significant contribution to the American judicial system. He worked diligently to streamline court procedures, improve efficiency, and enhance the Court's overall functioning. His legal acumen and dedication to the principles of fairness and impartiality left a lasting impact on the Supreme Court.

While Harding's presidency was overshadowed by scandals and criticized for its lack of effective governance, his selection of Taft as Chief Justice stands out as a testament to his ability to make sound decisions in the realm of judicial appointments. It underscores the importance of recognizing talent and expertise in shaping the highest echelons of the government.

Calvin Coolidge

Independence Day

The birthday of Calvin Coolidge, on 4 July 1872, was exactly 96 years after the Declaration of Independence which is generally regarded as the birthday of his country. I believe this coincidence influenced his personality and career.

Any one selected day of the year has slightly more than a 10% probability of being the birthday of any of the 39 Presidents. Therefore, a selective factor is suggested by the birth of this one President on the special day of 4 July.

More convincing evidence comes from a much larger sample, the Governors of the States, assuming that the same selective factor applied to them as to the Presidents. Among 1,712 Governors who took office in 1979 or earlier, ten were born on 4 July, including Coolidge, who was Governor of Massachusetts before he became President. This number is appreciably higher than the average of 4.7 Governors expected to be born on any selected day.

An augmented identification with the nation in a person born on Independence Day may increase the probability of choosing a political career. Additional votes for the candidate who shares the national birthday might help him to win elections. A stronger influence, in my opinion, is that birth on the national Independence Day contributes to a personal declaration of independence needed to attain high political offices. Comprehensive conformity to the social expectations, attempted by many people, is incompatible with outstanding achievement.

John Calvin Coolidge, Jr. declared his independence from social expectations in several ways. One was the omission of his first name. Another was avoidance of small talk and superficial joviality, although he was highly intelligent, an excellent writer, and an attractive person.

One of my nieces was born on 4 July 1973. I hope this essay on her birth date will encourage her to express independence in constructive ways, such as the outstanding achievement by President Coolidge, rather than in destructive ways, such as social withdrawal.

Herbert Hoover

Ambivalent About Ambiguity

You, the reader, probably know the exact day of the year you were born. Most of us learned this information at a very early age. It is an important part of our self-knowledge, which we will remember throughout life.

Herbert Clark Hoover was unusual in this respect. He was born near midnight on 10-11 August 1874. The records of the Quaker Church in West Branch, Iowa and Hoover's autobiographical account prepared about 1915 specify the 11th. Hoover's subsequent Memoirs and most of his biographers specify the 10th.

This initial ambiguity may have aggravated the effects of subsequent disturbances of his early development, notably the death of his father (when Herbert was six years old) and of his mother (when he was nine years old). His adult career manifested ambivalence about ambiguity. He disliked uncertainty and disorder, but he also sought and exploited these conditions.

He effectively controlled some aspects of his environment. He chose the precise, quantitative profession of engineering. He specialized in reorganizing unsuccessful companies. Strong, well-organized leadership accounted for his success as Chairman of the Commission for Relief in Belgium 1915-1918, U.S. Food Administrator 1917-1919, and U.S. Secretary of Commerce 1921-1928.

Seemingly inconsistent traits are explainable by his identification with ambiguity. His early career was in mining precious metals, which is a high-risk enterprise with a high proportion of failures. His published memoirs were very careless with facts and dates. He relied on others to attend to many of the details of his business and writing.

Hoover's combination of orderliness and ambiguity probably contributed to his nomination and election as President of the United States in 1928. His need for control, together with acceptance of ambiguity, attracted him to a political career and impelled him to the top. He was helped by his status as the Great Engineer and by his skillful use of the glittering generalities and pleasant platitudes that conceal the sentiments and intentions of politicians. The ambiguity about the day of the year he was born may be one of the reasons why he became President.

Franklin Delano Roosevelt

Dutiful Deceiver

Franklin Delano Roosevelt was born on 30 January 1882. Therefore, the first month of the 104th year afterwards is a suitable time for an essay about him. Insightful inferences, based on well-documented information, are communicated in an excellent biography, "Before the Trumpet; Young Franklin Roosevelt 1882-1905," by Geoffrey C. Ward (New York: Harper & Row 1985).

F.D.R. was dutiful and deceitful. These are generally opposing traits, one good and the other bad. In F.D.R., their origins were linked. Both traits contributed to his unique success as the only President of the United States elected for more than two terms.

He cultivated an appearance of being gregarious and fearless. Those who knew him best, including his wife, agreed that his inner feelings were mysterious and inaccessible to them. The only fear he acknowledged was of fire. This originated from a traumatic experience at the age of two and a half years. He was present when his nineteen-year-old aunt, Laura Delano, was fatally burned.

His sense of duty distinguished F.D.R. from the rich, self-indulgent boys he grew up with and also from the greedy, ambitious politicians he dealt with as an adult. His ardent desire was not only to become and remain President but also to do a good job. He staffed the government with idealistic, able people, and he expected them to do their duty.

The biographer, Geoffrey C. Ward, identifies some sources of F.D.R.'s dutiful deceit. Being brought up as the only child of rich, indulgent parents, he learned to be self-centered and manipulative. He formed a close attachment with his parents. Both of them had well-developed senses of duty, which included the deception of concealing or renouncing some of their feelings, such as erotic desire.

When F.D.R. was 12 years old, his father, who was 62, suffered a heart attack. Thereafter, until his father's death ten years later, F.D.R. felt that it was his duty to protect his father from grief and disappointment by being a good son, fulfilling his father's desires. His duty included deception, joining his mother in concealing from his father their anxiety about his health. Dutiful deceit, thus developed in adolescence, persisted throughout his political career.

91

Harry S. Truman

Surprise Winner

Harry S. Truman, the 32nd President of the United States, was born on May 8, 1884. Interestingly, his middle initial, "S," did not stand for any specific name but was chosen to honor both his grandfathers, Anderson Shipp Truman and Solomon Young. This was an unusual choice of name.

During World War I, Truman served as an outstanding commander of an artillery company in France from 1917 to 1919. His military experience and leadership skills contributed to his success on the battlefield, earning him the respect of his fellow soldiers.

Truman's political career began when he was elected as a U.S. Senator, serving from 1935 to 1945. His dedication to public service and his ability to navigate the complexities of politics caught the attention of President Franklin D. Roosevelt, who selected him as his third vice President in 1945.

Truman assumed the presidency following Roosevelt's death in April 1945. His tenure as President coincided with the end of World War II and the onset of the Cold War.

One of Truman's notable contributions to the Cold War was his involvement in the Korean War. Despite the challenges and complexities of the conflict, Truman's leadership and decision-making earned him praise from historians. His resolute stance against the Soviet Union and dedication to defending democratic values further solidified his reputation as a strong leader.

In the 1948 Presidential election, Truman defied expectations and emerged victorious against Republican nominee Dewey. This surprising outcome showcased Truman's political resilience and ability to connect with the American people. His leadership during the war and his commitment to addressing domestic issues endeared him to many voters.

Truman, aware of the newly imposed two-term limit for the presidency, chose not to seek re-election in 1952. This decision marked the end of his presidency, as Dwight D. Eisenhower, the Republican nominee, won the election that year. Truman's voluntary retirement from the office demonstrated his respect for the democratic principles and norms of the nation.

One decision that defined Truman's presidency was his authorization of the atomic bombings of Hiroshima and Nagasaki in August 1945. While this decision remains a topic of debate among historians, it undeniably brought a swift end to the war and solidified the United States' position as a global power. Truman's bold action has received both criticism and praise, with many historians recognizing the complexity and gravity of the circumstances he faced.

In retrospect, Truman is widely regarded as one of the best Presidents of the United States.

Dwight Eisenhower

Why We Liked Ike
October 1990

During October 1990, a full century will be completed since 14 October 1890, when Dwight David Eisenhower was born. His presidency of the United States, 1953-1961, is remembered as a peaceful interlude between the Korean War and the Vietnam War. His character and his performance in office helped to preserve the peace.

Eisenhower had a combination of contrasting traits: amiability and assertion. He is generally regarded as amiable rather than assertive. A prominent campaign slogan in 1952 was "I Like Ike." He was attractive and friendly in appearance and personality. His more impressive attributes were largely hidden from the public.

His dual traits of amiability and assertion were described well in the Memoirs of Richard Nixon (vol. 1, New York: Warner Books, 1979, pages 464-465). "Perhaps the best description I can give of Dwight Eisenhower is that he had a warm smile and icy blue eyes. It was not a case of being outwardly warm and inwardly cold. Rather, beneath his captivating personal appearance was a lot of finely tempered hard steel....While most people probably remembered him for his engaging, outgoing personality, I remember him for his decisive leadership."

Eisenhower's career displayed his strong assertiveness. He enrolled at the United States Military Academy, although both his parents were pacifists. His academic record as a cadet was not outstanding, but the evaluations of him at graduation time included the comment, "Born to command." His rise to the top in the army and in politics is attributable more to his impressive performance than to his charming personality.

He was skillful at reconciling diverse sentiments. An example, during the 1952 Presidential campaign, was his answer to a question by newspaper reporters whether he considered himself a conservative or a liberal. "I consider myself a conservative with respect to fiscal policies and a liberal with respect to human values."

His fiscal conservatism was bolstered by the honest, efficient subordinates whom he chose and managed. He avoided federal budget deficits, successfully withstanding demands from Congress and the public to decrease taxes and increase spending. He fulfilled his aim of cutting the fat but not the muscle from military budgets. He thereby curtailed military spending while improving the military capabilities. These policies benefitted the United States for many years after his presidency.

His liberal human values were expressed in conciliatory dealings with political allies and opponents. He defeated political extremists and racists by his tolerant spirit and by winning over many of their supporters rather than by provocative denunciations. An example was his comment about Senator Joseph McCarthy: "I will not get into the gutter with that guy." He appointed to the Supreme Court two of the most effective liberal Justices, Earl Warren and William J Brennan.

Assertion and amiability are contrasting traits, but they can occur together. Their concurrent strong presence in Dwight Eisenhower helped him to perform with great success as a military and political leader.

Framework for
Freedom

May 1995

Freedom is a desirable condition. A political application is the motto, "That government is best which governs least" (Henry David Thoreau in "Civil Disobedience" 1849). An economic application is the free market.

In common with most other desirable conditions, excessive freedom is toxic. Unlimited freedom is anarchy, which results in chaos. Beneficial freedom requires a framework of control. An example is the federal government's power to break up a monopolistic corporation in order to preserve competition in the free market.

In some cases, it is unclear and controversial whether a framework of control preserves or destroys freedom. An example is the proposal of term limits for legislators, part of Newt Gingrich's Contract with America. A constitutional amendment to limit the terms of the United States Congress was recently approved by the majority of members of the House of Representatives, but by less than the two thirds required for passage of the proposal. Many states have enacted term limits for their members of the United States Congress. The Supreme Court is scheduled to rule on the constitutionality of that restriction.

Term limits restrict the freedom of legislators to seek reelection and the freedom of voters to reelect them. The most experienced legislators become ineligible for election. The diversity of the legislature is impaired if all are novices. A further disadvantage is that rash, unwise laws might be enacted by legislators that do not include enough experienced, mature members.

It is possible to argue that term limits provide a framework of control that maximizes the freedom of voters to elect the preferable candidate. Without term limits, the advantages of incumbency might preclude the opponent from winning the election.

It is preferable to protect freedom by a framework of responsible choices rather than by a framework of restrictive laws. The choice between candidates in all elections is influenced by multiple attributes. Voters can counteract the advantage of incumbency by regarding long-term incumbency as an adverse attribute.

In the primary election, 16 May, Democratic voters in Allegheny County will have the opportunity to retain or replace incumbents Tom Foerster, seeking his eighth four-year term, and Pete Flaherty, seeking his fourth term. Their most active and best qualified opponents are Michael M. Dawida, serving his second term as a State Senator, and Coleen Vuono, and administrator in the County Coroner's Office and former President of the Mt. Lebanon Board of Commissioners. For Republican voters, the incumbent is Larry Dunn, seeking his second term. His running mate is Bob Cranmer; a well-qualified, feminist opponent is Linda Dickerson.

LIFE

'Any
dangerous
spot
is tenable
if brave men
will
make it so'

AUGUST 4 · 1961 · 20¢

John Fitzgerald Kennedy

The Brothers Kennedy

May 1986

John Fitzgerald Kennedy, born on 29 May 1917, is widely known to have been the second of four brothers. Some of the differences among the four are attributable to the combination of their different birth positions and their different names.

Joseph Patrick Kennedy, Jr., the first of nine children, was similar to his father, after whom he was named. He showed the ambition and aggressiveness typical of the firstborn. He often beat up his brother Jack but was kind and attentive toward the younger children. He was charming and impressive, but his rash, impetuous behavior would probably have blighted his political career even if he had survived World War II. For example, as a delegate to the Democratic National Convention in 1940, he voted against the nomination of Roosevelt for his third term, adhering to his father's sentiment in a politically foolish gesture.

The next child, Jack, was very diplomatic and popular in accordance with his birth position. He was given the name of his mother's father (John Francis Fitzgerald). This identification with his mother may have supplemented his masculinity with attributes of feminine identification, increasing his attractiveness to both sexes. His name also probably enhanced his identification with his maternal grandfather, a popular politician nicknamed Honey Fitz.

The third son, Robert Francis, explained his extraordinary competitiveness by the statement, "I was the seventh of nine children, and when you come from that far down you have to struggle to survive." He was not named after a family member. His middle name, which was not on his birth certificate and was chosen subsequently, was also the middle name of his maternal grandfather.

Edward Moore Kennedy, the last of the nine, was named after Eddie Moore, a loyal assistant of his father. Ted's behavior and political career express his conflict between renouncing and enjoying his indulged, immature status as the baby of the family. He is impressively eloquent and likable but also self-indulgent and self-destructive.

The birth positions and names contribute to our knowledge about the brothers Kennedy. Their differential attributes include Joe Jr.'s exalted reputation, Jack's attractiveness, Bobby's competitiveness, Ted's political skills and erratic behavior.

'STICK 'EM UP!'

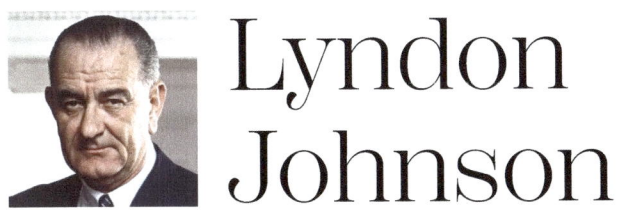

Lyndon Johnson

Tormented Texan

Texas affiliation is a source of both pride and anxiety. Texans share in the expansiveness of their large state with its traditions of great size and achievement. Anxiety is generated in Texans who are afraid they will fail to fulfill the state's proud traditions.

The pride and anxiety of Texans were both expressed by Lyndon Baines Johnson, who was born in Stonewall, Texas, on 27 August 1908. He had the advantages of large physical stature and extraordinary energy, ambition, and achievements. Nevertheless, he was tormented by anxiety over his failures to fulfill the ideals of Texas.

He identified with his tall, assertive, crude father. His masculine identification was accompanied, however, by an unusually strong identification with his beautiful, well-educated, gracious mother. His middle name was the premarital surname of his mother. She was disappointed in the mediocre achievements of her husband and focused her ambitions on Lyndon, their first child.

The son acquired from his mother a high degree of intelligence and esthetic sensitivity. He was tormented by the conflict between these attributes and the boisterous Texan masculinity he displayed.

Indications of Lyndon Johnson's torment included his cardiovascular failures and his reactions to them. At the age of 46 years, while Majority Leader of the United States Senate, he suffered a severe heart attack. Several months later he resumed his extravagantly heavy schedule of duties and activities. He died of another heart attack at the relatively early age of 65 years.

Lyndon Johnson's torment is evident in his exaggerated desire for control over domestic and foreign events while he was President of the United States from 1963-69. He felt compelled to win what many wise Americans viewed as an unwinnable war in Vietnam. His intelligent perception of the situation contributed to his torment and induced him to initiate the peace talks that ultimately ended the war.

Many people commented that President Johnson's escalation of the war in 1965 was the same policy as advocated by Barry Goldwater, his opponent in the 1964 Presidential election. Goldwater remarked that he would have done the same thing but would have enjoyed it more. Johnson's torment was preferable to the prospective President Goldwater's enjoyment of the military escalation.

Richard Nixon

Anguish About Anger

Some people's characters and lives are dominated by a distinctive fault. Anger was the dominating fault of Richard Milhous Nixon. His anger was revealed by many of his words, physical gestures, and decisions. Awareness of these signs accounts for the intense hostility toward him by many voters and political colleagues. He reciprocated fully their hostility. This adverse interaction led to the actions by Nixon that resulted in his resignation as President of the United States in August 1974.

A recurrent theme in fictional tragedies is the fatal fault that destroys a person with outstanding abilities and achievements. Reality is more complex than fiction. Anger did not completely overwhelm Nixon. He benefited from constructive influences, including the strong, admirable characters of his parents. His highly developed self-control enabled him to conceal and counteract most expressions of his anger. He had benign emotions, including love for his family members, affiliations with friends, and patriotic loyalty to his country. His very keen, analytical mind helped him to obtain respect and many successes.

The disgrace of Richard Nixon in 1974 was followed by almost fatal blood clots that originated from inflammation of veins in the leg. These tragic afflictions were fortunately not the final events of his life. He recovered from the illness. For more than 19 years afterward, he wrote important books and gave good advice to his successors.

Richard Milhous Nixon's anger was a primitive emotion, originating in early childhood. I believe that he felt rejected by his pious Quaker mother, Hannah Milhous Nixon. For him, she was supremely important and the model for many of his traits. He shared her premarital surname. For her, he was the second of five sons, all of whom were less important than her loving and beloved husband.

Another contribution to Richard Nixon's anger was disapproval of his own kinder, gentler nature. His low self-esteem induced the self-destructiveness of some of his political decisions. He craved to be an athletic, assertive, aggressive, confident man.

We admire people who overcome severe physical or social obstacles. We can also admire Richard Milhous Nixon, whose constructive achievements overcame his destructive fault of chronic, intense feelings of anger.

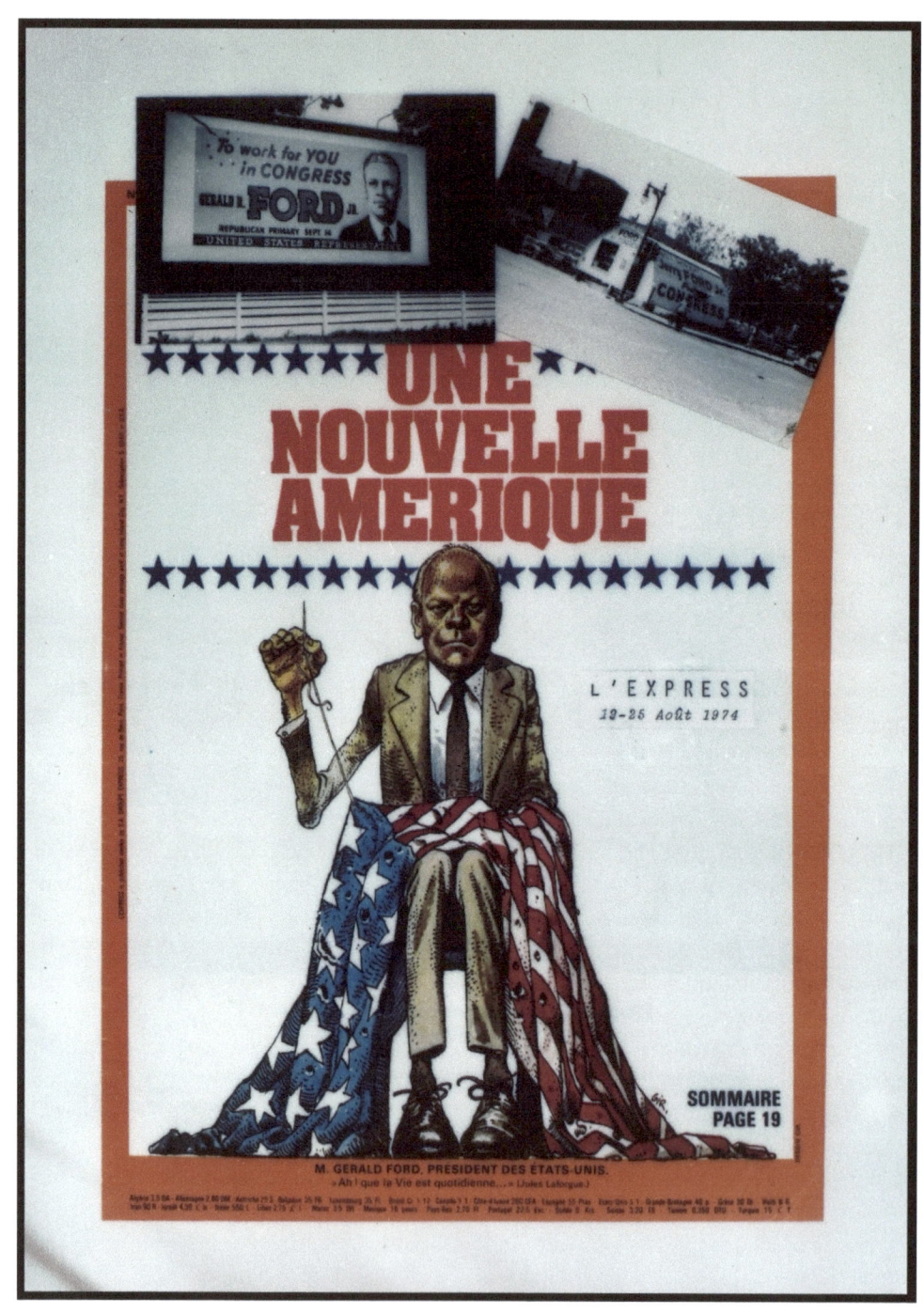

Gerald Ford

Bastille Bash Bicentennial

The interval of exactly 200 years on 14 July 1989 will induce a special celebration of Bastille Day. This important French holiday commemorates an early event of the French Revolution when a crowd stormed the Bastille and released the prisoners on 14 July 1789.

A concurrent American anniversary is the 76th birthday of Gerald Ford, former President of the United States, who was born on 14 July 1913. The special significance of Ford's birthday might have influenced his personality development and choice of career toward politics and international relations. Although Bastille Day was not a holiday for the residents of Grand Rapids, Michigan, he undoubtedly became aware at an early age that his birthday was a memorable date, reproduced in textbooks of modern European history.

Gerald Ford's fifth birthday, in 1918, coincided with a time when American soldiers were fighting as allies of the French in their country. His parents were probably aware then of the special significance of his birth date, whether or not the small boy was given this information. In subsequent years, Gerald Ford might have developed a greater interest in national and international events because of his personal connection with an important date in European history.

The birthday of another President of the United States coincides with the anniversary of the American Revolution. Calvin Coolidge was born on 4 July 1872. A notable fact about both Coolidge and Ford is that although their birthdays are associated with famous revolutions, their doctrines were not reformist, radical, or rebellious. Their political activities as members of the conservative Republican party might have been stimulated by their awareness of the destructive violence associated with their birthdays.

The births of two conservative Presidents coinciding with the anniversaries of famous revolutions might be coincidences due to random chance. It is evident, however, that a combination of improbable events accounts for a particular individual being the one among millions of eligible citizens to become President of the United States. These improbable events might include the unusual significance of the date of birth of President Coolidge on 4 July and of President Ford on 14 July.

THE ICEMAN COMETH

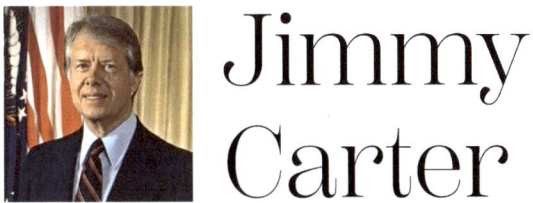

Jimmy Carter

Son of James Earl, Senior

A boy learns two contrasting responses toward his father: identification with him and differentiation from him. In my opinion, a boy who shares the same first name as the father usually develops exaggerated intensity of both responses.

Jimmy Carter, who was born on 1 October 1924, shares all three components of his father's name. His official name is James Earl Carter, Jr. He displays identification with his father by loyalty to his father's affiliations and traditions. He is differentiated from his father by additional loyalty and humanitarian values.

James Earl Carter, Senior, was consistently loyal to the United States, to the Baptist church, to this community, and to his family. His son Jimmy shows the same loyalties. The son's emphasis on loyalty is indicated by the title he chose for his memoirs of his presidency, "Keeping Faith."

Loyalty is expressed not only by sentiments but also by diligent service. James Earl Carter worked hard and effectively for his country, church, community, and family. His son Jimmy surpasses his father in his diligent service. For example, his impressively sustained efforts made possible his campaigns for election as a State Senator, as the Governor of Georgia, and as the President of the United States.

Jimmy Carter's differentiation from his father is manifested by his loyal and diligent service to humanitarian values. His father was a conservative who did not advocate humanitarian reforms. The son's admiration of President Franklin D. Roosevelt, beginning in childhood, differentiated him from his father's political sentiments. The son became a vigorous opponent of racial segregation, contrary to the sentiments of his father and most of their white neighbors.

Fervent and diligent loyalty to humanitarian values contributed to Jimmy Carter's outstanding achievements during his presidency from 1977-1981 and subsequently. These achievements include his advocacy of the two Panama Canal treaties, his mediation of the Camp David Accords by Sadat and Begin, and his negotiations for the release of the American hostages in Iran at the end of his presidency. Afterward, he contributed greatly to Habitat for Humanity and to conflict resolution and other programs at the Carter Presidential Center. All human beings have thereby benefited from Jimmy Carter's intense identification with and differentiation from his father.

RICHARD NIXON

August 13, 1987

26 FEDERAL PLAZA
NEW YORK CITY

CJ

No Reply phone

533859
5200
SP1169
FG002·36
PR007·02
PR005·02

Dear Ron,

The speech last night was one of your best.
What was even more important than what you said was
that you sounded and looked strong. You gave the
lie to the crap about your being over-the-hill,
discouraged, etc.

If I could be permitted one word of advice:
Don't ever comment on the Iran-Contra matter again.
Have instructions issued to all White House
staffers and Administration spokesmen that they must
never answer any question on or off the record
about that issue in the future. They should reply
to all inquiries by stating firmly and
categorically that the President has addressed the
subject and that they have nothing to add.

The committee labored for nine months and
produced a stillborn midget. Let it rest in peace!

Sincerely,

Dick

The Honorable
Ronald Reagan

108

Ronald Regan

Peculiar Past President

The word peculiar means special or strange. This is an accurate description of the status of Ronald Reagan as the past President of the United States, whose successor is a member of the same party. The last previous occurrence was 60 years ago.

This event, peculiar in recent American history, was frequent in earlier years. A past President was succeeded by a member of his party ten previous times in 132 years, beginning when Washington became the first past President in 1797. The subsequent occasions were Jefferson (1809), Madison (1817), Monroe (1825), Jackson (1837), Pierce (1857), Grant (1877), Hayes (1881), T. Roosevelt (1909), and Coolidge (1929), followed by the long interval of 60 years until 1989.

This list of previous past Presidents includes some of the greatest and some of the worst in the opinions of most historians. Those who chose or apparently preferred their successor are highly regarded by most historians: Washington, Jefferson, Jackson, and T. Roosevelt. Those whose successor was chosen by their party rather than by themselves are less respected by historians: Madison, Monroe, Pierce, Grant, Hayes, and Coolidge.

Reagan was followed as President by a member of his party, whom he chose as his vice President and apparently preferred as his successor. This political triumph is a peculiar distinction, whatever is the future judgment of other aspects of his performance. The next several decades will determine whether the long interval of 60 years since the retiring President was followed by a member of his party has been an unusual interlude or the beginning of a new trend in the succession of Presidents.

When the past President has been followed by a member of his party, the successor in most cases has not fared well in that office. These successors are J. Adams (1797-1801), Madison (1809-17), Monroe (1817-25), J. Q. Adams (1825-29), Van Buren (1837-41), Buchanan (1857-61), Hayes (1877-81), Garfield (1881), Taft (1909-13), and Hoover (1929-33). Only two of these ten Presidents were reelected. If Bush has a successful presidency, his achievement will be peculiar in the same sense as Reagan's status as a past President whose successor is a member of his party.

George HW Bush

The Names of President Bush

George Herbert Walker Bush, born on 12 June 1924, is the only President of the United States whose birthday is in June. In comparison with the other Presidents, his names are unusual in some respects and typical in other respects.

The first name, George, is enduringly popular and shared with George Washington and King George III. It is remarkable that Bush is the first repetition of George after the first President. George is the first name of three vice Presidents: George Clinton, 1805-1812; George Mifflin Dallas, 1845-1849; and George Herbert Walker Bush, 1981-1989.

Among Presidents and vice Presidents of the United States, the only prior occurrence of multiple middle names was Vice President William Rufus De Vane King, 1853. Multiple middle names are prevalent in the British royal family but continue to be rare among the general population.

George Herbert Walker was the name of the maternal grandfather of President Bush. The names of the mother's father were reproduced in the first two names of two prior Presidents: Thomas Woodrow Wilson and John Fitzgerald Kennedy.

The surname, Bush, has English antecedents in common with the surnames of most of the Presidents. Contrary to most surnames, Bush is a word in the contemporary language. Contemporary words are also the surnames of prior Presidents Pierce, Grant, Ford, and Carter and of prior Vice Presidents Burr, King, and Wheeler. Among these, Burr and Bush are the only words that refer to tangible objects.

The name George is probably a political asset. In addition to its association with the first President, the single syllable has a sound of powerful masculinity. Most first names are two syllables; one-syllable names are usually given to boys, while names with more than two syllables are usually given to girls. This attribute of the name George may have helped to counteract his wimp image while he was vice President and a candidate for President.

The two middle names are probably a political liability. Accordingly, they are seldom publicized. Even single middle names have generally not been publicized by the most recent Presidents: Richard Milhous Nixon, Gerald Rudolph Ford, James Earl Carter, and Ronald Wilson Reagan.

The first middle name, Herbert, is old-fashioned. It has declined in popularity during the last several decades. The present writer is well aware of this fact, having the same name as both his father and grandfather Herbert.

President Bush was undoubtedly aware from an early age that his second middle name, Walker, reproduces his mother's premarital surname. This awareness probably intensified his maternal identification, especially because his father's name was reproduced in his older brother, Prescott S. Bush, Jr. Many boys counteract an unusually strong maternal identification by exaggerated masculine assertiveness. This is evident in the behavior of George Herbert Walker Bush and also of several recent Presidents of the United States whose middle names also reproduce their mother's premarital surname. In addition to Franklin Delano Roosevelt and John Fitzgerald Kennedy, these are Thomas Woodrow Wilson, Lyndon Baines Johnson, Richard Milhous Nixon, and Ronald Wilson Reagan.

Vice Presidents in Presidential Elections

November 1988

A candidate for vice President of the United States has two functions, which are inconsistent with each other. One function, to be the potential replacement for the President, implies that the vice President should resemble him or her. The Latin word vice means "in the place of." The other function, to enlarge the support for both candidates, explains why the Presidential candidate often selects somebody with contrasting characteristics. The differences between the two candidates thereby balance the ticket.

Several differences between the Presidential and vice-Presidential candidates this year indicate balancing of the ticket. The two Democrats are from Massachusetts in the northeast and Texas in the southwest, as in 1960. The conservative Democrats are represented by the vice-Presidential candidate while the liberal Democrats are represented by the Presidential candidate.

The Republican ticket is balanced in other ways. Indiana, the home of the vice-Presidential candidate, is approximately halfway between the Presidential candidate's official residence in Texas and his principal home in Maine. A large age difference between the two Republicans constitutes another type of contrast.

The tickets are also balanced by personality differences between the Presidential and vice-Presidential candidates. The childhood family environment is one of the sources of adult personality. The two Presidential candidates resemble each other and differ from the vice-Presidential candidates in this formative experience.

Both Presidential candidates grew up with an older brother named after their father, while the mother's family is commemorated in the names of the younger brothers who are now Presidential candidates. Both candidates learned at an early age to compete successfully with the older brother, to feel closely affiliated with the mother and less fearful of the father's authority, and to achieve independently of the paternal family tradition.

Both vice Presidential candidates have the same first name as the father. This paternal affiliation increased their subordination to their father during childhood and their adherence to tradition and their deference to authority figures in adulthood. The personalities of the vice-Presidential candidates this year fulfill the function of balancing the tickets rather than resembling the Presidential candidates.

THE WHITE HOUSE

WASHINGTON

Jan 20, 1993

Dear Bill,

When I walked into this office just now I felt the same sense of wonder and respect that I felt four years ago. I know you will feel that, too.

I wish you great happiness here. I never felt the loneliness some Presidents have described.

There will be very tough times, made even more difficult by criticism you may not think is fair. I'm not a very good one to give advice; but just don't let the critics discourage you or push you off course.

You will be <u>our</u> President when you read this note. I wish you well. I wish your family well.

Your success now is our country's success. I am rooting hard for you.

Good Luck – George

George Bush Presidential Library and Museum

William Jefferson Clinton

William Jefferson Clinton was the forty-first President, elected in 1992 against the incumbent President George H W Bush, who was criticized for breaking his promise not to raise taxes. He won two terms and had many accomplishments, including helping to end the war in the Balkans, a period of strong economic growth, and the North American Free Trade Block, including Canada and Mexico.

Despite these successes, he is best remembered today for his impeachment at the end of his second term.

Questions of his fidelity to his marriage appeared in his first campaign, but the testimony during the impeachment, which lasted 7 months, captured the attention of the country. He was impeached by the House of Representatives and then acquitted by the Senate and completed the remaining few months of his presidency.

Andrew Johnson was the only other President impeached by the House of Representatives and only escaped being convicted by the Senate by one vote. Johnson, who was Abraham Lincoln's Vice President, fought with Congress over the Reconstruction and the authority of the President. Clinton's impeachment was for lying under oath and obstruction of justice, but the cause was his affair with Monica Lewinski, a White House intern.

Clinton was not the first President to be accused of extramarital affairs. Franklin Delano Roosevelt reportedly had an affair with a Norwegian Princess. There were 15 other Presidents that have been accused of sexual misconduct. The accusations range from having a serious sexual relationship outside of marriage (Washington, Lincoln, Wilson and Roosevelt) to fathering a child out of wedlock (Jefferson and Cleveland) to having one or more extramarital affairs (Harding, Eisenhower, Kennedy, Johnson, Bush and Clinton).

Many of the stories involving Presidents were also sensational. Thomas Jefferson had two children with a slave from his plantation during his first term. John Kennedy reportedly had an affair with Marilyn Monroe, the movie star. George HW Bush was accused of having an affair with a White House staffer. Lyndon B Johnson's biography wrote that when people mentioned Kennedy's affairs, he would bang on the table and say he had more women by accident than Kennedy had on purpose

The key difference for Clinton was that the accusations were made public while he was in office and that the investigation led to questions of his conduct overall. For many politicians, accusations of sexual misconduct would ruin their chances of election. Chester A. Arthur, the twenty-first President in the 1880s, was accused of having a mistress while he was running for a second term and said he considered the accusation worse than assassination. That is markedly different from today. Donald Trump, while running for President, was able to ignore multiple lawsuits and a public recording of his bad behavior with women and still be elected in 2016.

George W. Bush

Questionable Decision

The election between George Bush and Al Gore in 2000 was especially close, and I believe it was won by the wrong candidate.

Vice President Gore was the Democratic nominee in the year President Clinton was almost impeached by the Republican majority in Congress. Gore lost an extremely close election. Bush was the Republican nominee.

When Bush entered politics, he was in his late forties and felt he had accomplished very little in Dallas, Texas. He had been the principal cheerleader for the football team at Yale as an undergraduate, and he had a very good marriage and two twin daughters, but his business ventures in oil and gas were only a limited success. In his thirties he drank heavily and attended many parties with Republican sports leaders in Dallas.

He decided at 40 years old, before going into politics, that he would give up intoxicating beverages such as alcohol. In 1989, after working on his father's Presidential campaign, he led an investment group that bought the Texas Rangers. He was elected governor of Texas from 1995 until he resigned to run for President. In 2000, he won the Republican nomination for President of the United States.

The Democratic nominee, Al Gore, had been the Vice President. During the campaign, both candidates focused on how to maintain the strong economy. George W. Bush emphasized tax cuts as a way to stimulate economic growth, arguing that reducing taxes would benefit businesses and individuals, leading to increased investment and job opportunities. Al Gore proposed targeted tax cuts and investments in areas such as education, healthcare, and the environment. He highlighted the need for fiscal responsibility and advocated for using the budget surplus to invest in key domestic programs.

In an extremely close election, the decision rested on contested vote counting in the State of Florida. The governor of Florida was Jeb Bush, George Bush's brother. After multiple recounts, court cases were referred to the U.S. Supreme Court questioning if the State of Florida could continue doing county by county recounts.

The majority of the Supreme Court was Conservative and two justices had been appointed by George HW Bush, George W Bush's father. The court decided that the recounts were unconstitutional because they violated the Equal Protection Clause of the Fourteenth Amendment. The Court held that the recount procedures in Florida were inconsistent and lacked clear standards for determining voter intent, resulting in a violation of equal protection under the law. Since the first results had placed Bush as the winner of the state, he won the presidency.

Early in his presidency, in 2001, an aerial attack on three buildings in Washington and New York was conducted by Bin Laden. The Republican administration retaliated by declaring war on Afghanistan and Iraq. This precipitated many years of warfare. The aggressive response of President Bush was generally supported by most Americans. In 2004, Bush was reelected President for a second four-year term.

The second term for George W Bush, 2005-2009, was disastrous. A severe recession began in 2008. President Bush did nothing to reverse it. The President-elect, Barrack Obama, was forced to immediately engage and work to counteract the recession. George W Bush, therefore, was no longer effective. The recession was ended, and Osama Bin Laden was assassinated by Obama's administration.

Barack Hussein Obama

Barack Obama, the 43rd President of the United States, made history when he was elected as the Democratic nominee for President. This significant achievement was a moment of progress for the nation.

Barack Obama's name carries significance and has been the subject of public discussion. His middle name, Hussein, sparked curiosity and occasionally drew controversy. While some noted he did not use his middle name frequently, when asked, he said he embraced his full name with pride, emphasizing the importance of embracing one's identity and heritage.

When Obama secured the nomination, he made the announcement that he had chosen Joseph Biden as his running mate for the Vice Presidency. This decision showcased Obama's astute judgment and his commitment to assembling a strong and diverse team. With Biden by his side, Obama embarked on a transformative journey to the White House.

Biden's role as Vice President under Obama's administration spanned two four-year terms. Over the course of those eight years, a remarkable friendship developed between the two men. Biden, who spent considerable time in the White House, not only provided steadfast support but also became a trusted friend to Obama. Their bond endured even after Obama's presidency came to an end, demonstrating the lasting impact of their partnership.

The Obama-Biden era, which lasted from 2009 to 2017, was characterized by a spirit of cooperation and collaboration. Together, they tackled numerous challenges and pursued a progressive agenda.

One notable accomplishment during their tenure was the establishment of marriage equality, recognizing same-sex marriage as a legal partnership. While Biden expressed support for marriage equality early on, Obama initially supported civil unions as an alternative to marriage for same-sex couples. However, in 2012, he publicly announced his support for same-sex marriage, becoming the first sitting U.S. President to do so.

In a poignant moment at the end of their second term in 2016, President Obama surprised the nation by awarding his Vice President, Joseph R. Biden, with the Medal of Freedom, the highest civilian award in the United States. This well-conceived gesture of appreciation highlighted the deep respect and admiration Obama held for Biden's dedicated service as Vice President. The moment symbolized not only their professional collaboration but also the personal bond they had forged over the years.

Throughout his presidency, Obama demonstrated a commitment to progress. His leadership style and ability to inspire hope resonated with millions of Americans and people around the world. The legacy of the Obama-Biden administration continues to be celebrated as they navigated challenges, advanced social justice causes, and worked to uplift the nation.

Donald John Trump

The Worst President

The Republican nominee, Donald Trump, was elected as the 44th President for a single term from 2017 to 2021.

Trump broke several precedents during his campaign and his single term as President.

Unlike previous Presidents, he did not have a legal or military background. He was a real estate developer. Trump's father had amassed wealth buying and developing apartments in the boroughs of Brooklyn and Queens in New York City. Trump himself owned hotels and casinos in New York and Atlantic City, New Jersey.

Before his presidency, Trump gained popularity through hosting the TV show "The Apprentice," where he famously used the catchphrase "You're Fired!" when eliminating contestants. During his campaign for the Republican nomination, he successfully employed belittling tactics against his competitors, including Jeb Bush. Many feel Trump won the nomination by successfully appealing to white supremacists and gun owners in small communities.

In the 2016 Presidential election, Trump won several states with smaller populations, while his opponent, Hillary Clinton, secured most of the populous northern and coastal states. In the popular vote, Clinton had 2.9 million more votes, but Trump carried Pennsylvania, Michigan, and Wisconsin which meant he won the Electoral College. In 2020, when Joe Biden defeated Trump, Biden won the election by the same margin that Clinton had lost four years prior.

As President, Trump displayed a preference for dictators like Vladimir Putin of Russia and Kim Jong Un of North Korea. He also voiced concerns about excessive spending on U.S. troops in Europe and sought to reduce NATO expenditures, although this has been overwhelmingly reversed after the subsequent invasion of Ukraine which garnered bipartisan support for NATO and the defense of Ukraine.

Trump established a cordial relationship with Kim Jong Un, visiting North Korea, but this did not prevent North Korea from developing and testing intercontinental ballistic missiles. His main accomplishment was reducing taxes for corporations.

In his 2000 campaign against Joe Biden, he behaved badly in the first Presidential debate against Joe Biden frequently interrupting and breaking the rules set by the moderator. The second debate between the Presidential candidates was canceled. In the third Presidential debate, his behavior was better.

After the 2020 election, Trump attempted unsuccessfully to challenge the results.

Instead of attending Biden's inauguration, he departed for his residence in Mar-a-Lago, Florida, a day earlier. Other Presidents have not attended their successor's inaugurations. John Adams, in 1801, did not attend Thomas Jefferson's inauguration in what was the first peaceful transfer of power between parties in the country's history. John Quincy Adams, in 1829, and Andrew Johnson, in 1869, both did not attend because they had bitter and contentious relationships with their following Presidents.

Historians who will rank each President on their performance are most likely to rank him as the worst of all the Presidents.

Best wishes
To my friend Joe Biden
Jimmy Carter

Joe Robinette Biden, JR

Age and Experience

Joe Biden, the current President of the United States, was born Joseph Robinette Biden, Jr.

Biden, like other recent Presidents, has chosen not to extensively publicize his middle name. Other Presidents, such as Barack Hussein Obama, James Earl Carter, and George Herbert Walker Bush, also did not emphasize their middle names. The decision to downplay middle names may be attributed to personal preferences or the desire to focus on their primary identity as leaders rather than family names.

This apprehension is not uncommon among vice Presidents, as history has shown that the path to the presidency from the vice presidency is not assured.

Of the 15 vice Presidents who eventually assumed the presidency, only six were elected to the position. Eight assumed office due to the death of the President they served under, and the last, Gerald Ford, was never elected to the Executive Branch at all. He was appointed Vice President in 1973 and then was made President after the resignation of Nixon in 1974. Since Richard Nixon, the only vice president who successfully transitioned to the presidency through election was George H. W. Bush, and then Joe Biden.

Before his vice presidency, Biden made his mark as one of the youngest individuals to be elected to the United States Senate. At the age of 29, his election to the Senate showcased his early political acumen and set the stage for his future career in public service.

During the 2020 presidential campaign, Biden was not getting traction until his victory in South Carolina. With its large population of African Americans, this victory helped put him in the lead, particularly against Vermont senator Bernie Sanders. This reflects the relationship Biden had built with Barack Obama as Vice President.

A notable aspect of President Biden's presidency is his age. At 78 years old, he became the oldest person ever elected to the office of the President of the United States. This surpasses the previous record held by President Ronald Reagan, who was 69 years old when elected. Biden's age has sparked discussions about generational leadership and the unique perspectives and experiences he brings to the presidency.

About the Author

Dr. Herbert Barry III: A Pioneer
in Psychopharmacology

Dr. Herbert Barry III is a professor emeritus of pharmaceutical sciences at the University of Pittsburgh School of Pharmacy. He is a pioneer in the field of psychopharmacology, and his research has had a significant impact on our understanding of the effects of drugs on behavior.

Dr. Barry received his B.A. in Social Relations from Harvard College in 1955 and his M.S. and Ph.D. degrees in Psychology from Yale University in 1957 and 1959, respectively. He joined the faculty of the University of Pittsburgh School of Pharmacy in 1963.

Dr. Barry's research has focused on the effects of drugs on behavior, particularly the effects of psychotropic drugs on learning, memory, and aggression. He has published over 200 articles in peer-reviewed journals, and his work has been funded by the National Institutes of Health, the American Psychological Association, and the American Association for the Advancement of Science.

Dr. Barry is a Fellow of the American Association for the Advancement of Science, the American Psychological Association, and the American Association of Pharmaceutical Sciences. He is also a past President of the Division of Psychopharmacology of the American Psychological Association.

Dr. Barry is a highly respected researcher and educator who has made significant contributions to the field of psychopharmacology. His work has helped us to understand the effects of drugs on behavior, and it has led to the development of new treatments for a variety of psychiatric disorders.

In addition to his research, Dr. Barry has also been a strong advocate for the education of students and professionals in the field of psychopharmacology. He has served as a mentor to many students and colleagues, and he has been a tireless advocate for the advancement of the field.

Dr. Barry is a true pioneer in the field of psychopharmacology. His research has had a profound impact on our understanding of the effects of drugs on behavior, and his work has led to the development of new treatments for a variety of psychiatric disorders. He is a highly respected researcher, educator, and advocate for the field of psychopharmacology.

Awards and Honors

Fellow of the American Association for the Advancement of Science

Fellow of the American Psychological Association

Fellow of the American Association of Pharmaceutical Sciences

President of the Division of Psychopharmacology of the American Psychological Association

Recipient of an NIMH Post-Doctoral Fellowship at Yale University

Recipient of an NIMH Research Scientist Development Award

Author or co-author of more than 200 publications on diverse topics

Managing Editor and Field Editor of the Journal Psychopharmacology 1974-1991

Selected Books by Dr. Herbert Barry III

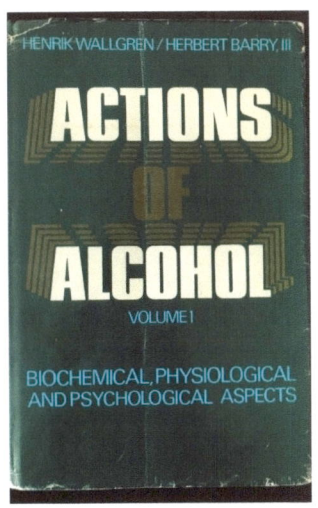

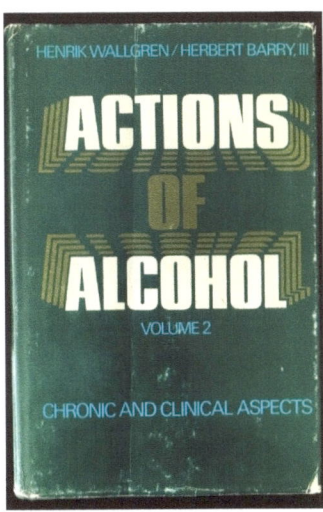

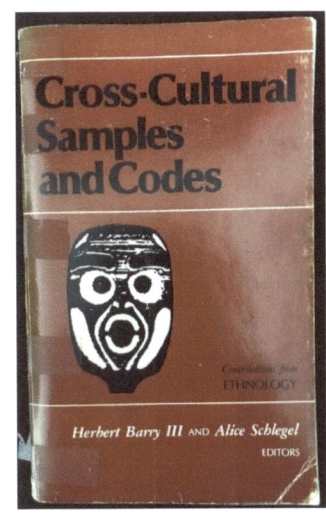

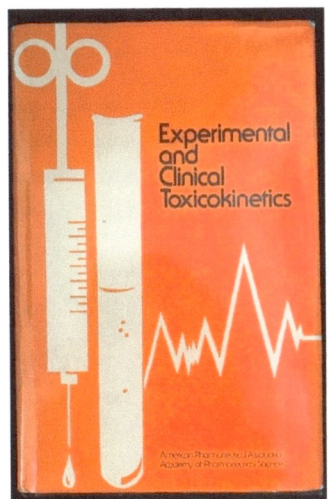

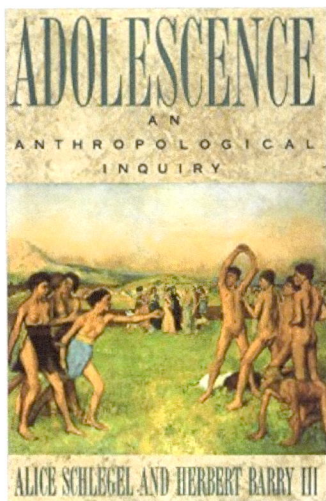

Published Articles

The Proximity of Paired Nations Reveals Correlation of Masculinity With Individualism, Feb 2015, Herbert Barry III

Racial and Gender Differences in Diversity of First Names, Mar 2010, Herbert Barry III, Aylene S Harper

Names in the Hebrew Bible, Dec 2007, Herbert Barry III, Jared J. Jackson

Final Letter Compared with Final Phoneme in Male and Female Names, Mar 2003, Herbert Barry III, Aylene S. Harper

Inference of Personality Projected onto Fictional Characters Having an Author's First Name, Jan 2002, Herbert Barry III

Research on First Names by Two Psychologists, Dec 2001, Herbert Barry III, Aylene S. Harper

Three Last Letters Identify Most Female First Names, Sep 2000, Herbert Barry III, AYLENE S. HARPER

Creation and First 20 Years of the Society for the Stimulus Properties of Drugs (SSPD), Nov 1999, Donald Overton, John Adam Rosecrans, Herbert Barry III

One experience with 'lower' or 'higher' intensity stressors, respectively enhances or diminishes responsiveness to haloperidol weeks later: implications for understanding drug variability, Jan 1992, Seymour M. Antelman, Anthony R. Caggiula, Donna Kocan, Herbert Barry III

100 volumes of Psychopharmacology, Mar 1990, Herbert Barry III, Trevor Robbins

The Effects of SKF 525-A on the Analgesic and Barbiturate-Potentiating Activity of Δ9Tetrahydrocannabinol in Mice and Rats, Feb 1983, R. D. Sofia, Herbert Barry III

Predictors of Longevity of United States Presidents, Jan 1983, Herbert Barry III

Evolution of Unisex Names, Mar 1982, Herbert Barry III, Aylene S. Harper

Bioavailability and Dissolution Behavior of Trisulfapyrimidine Suspensions, Jun 1979, L K Mathur, J M Jaffe, R I Poust, John Colaizzi

Birth positions of alcoholics, Jun 1977, Herbert Barry III, Howard Blane

The correlation between personality and the risk of alcoholism, Jan 1977, Herbert Barry III

Sex of Siblings of Male Alcoholics, Dec 1975, Howard Blane, Herbert Barry III

Birth Order and Alcoholism; a Review, Sep 1973, Howard Blane, Herbert Barry III

Enhanced Pseudoephedrine Absorption by Concurrent Administration of Aluminum Hydroxide Gel in Humans, Jun 1972, Richard Lucarotti, John Colaizzi, Herbert Barry III, Rolland I. Poust

Birth order as a method of studying environmental influences in alcoholism, Jun 1972, Herbert Barry III, Howard Blane

Value of Repeated Tests in a Percutaneous Absorption Study, Feb 1972, Herbert Barry III, Fred Marcus, John Colaizzi

Sex Differences in Birth Order of Alcoholics, Jan 1972, Howard Blane, Herbert Barry III

Effects of Dietary Components on GI Absorption of Acetaminophen Tablets in Man, Nov 1971, James M. Jaffe, John Colaizzi, Herbert Barry III, Herbert Barry III

Published Articles

Infancy and Early Childhood: Cross-Cultural Codes 2, Oct 1971, Herbert Barry III, Leonora M. Paxson

Widely Used Drug. (Book Reviews: Actions of Alcohol. Vol. 1, Biochemical, Physiological and Psychological Aspects. Vol. 2, Chronic and Clinical Aspects), Jan 1971, Henrik Wallgren, Herbert Barry III

The Psychology of Space Travel: A Study of Astronaut Adaptation, Sep 1962, Herbert Barry III

The Predictability of Criminal Behavior, May 1962, Herbert Barry III

A Cross-Cultural Study of Sexual Behavior, Jan 1962, Irvin L. Child, Margaret K. Bacon, Herbert Barry III

The Role of Learning in Recovery from Schizophrenia, Sep 1961, Herbert Barry III

Cross-Cultural Aspects of Puberty Rituals, Mar 1961, Herbert Barry III

The Cross-Cultural Study of Psychotic Reactions, Jun 1960, Herbert Barry III

Temporal Factors in the Discrimination of Successive Auditory Stimuli, May 1960, Irvin L. Child, Herbert Barry III

Cross-Cultural Studies of Social Interaction, Jan 1960, Herbert Barry III, Margaret K. Bacon

The Differentiation of Discriminative Responses with Reinforcement Patterns, Nov 1959, Herbert Barry III

Temporal Effects in the Discrimination of Successive Auditory Stimuli, May 1959, Herbert Barry III, Irvin L. Child

Sensory Adaptation and Signal Detection in the Visual Field, Mar 1959, Herbert Barry III

The Relationship between Time and Reinforcement in the Differentiation of Discriminative Responses, Sep 1958, Herbert Barry III

The Effects of Alcohol on the Discrimination of Visual and Auditory Stimuli, Jun 1958, Herbert Barry III

Cross-Cultural Studies of Drinking and Drug Use, Apr 1958, Herbert Barry III, Margaret K. Bacon, Irvin L. Child

Prediction of Visual Thresholds with Time and Frequency of Stimulation, Nov 1957, Herbert Barry III

A Cross-Cultural Study of Drinking and Drug Use, Nov 1957, Herbert Barry III, Margaret K. Bacon, Irvin L. Child

The Discrimination of Successive Visual Stimuli, May 1957, Herbert Barry III, Irvin L. Child

Time Factors in Auditory Signal Detection, May 1957, Irvin L. Child, Herbert Barry III

The Discrimination of Successive Auditory Stimuli, Mar 1957, Herbert Barry III, Irvin L. Child

The Relationship between the Duration of a Stimulus and Its Discriminability, Nov 1956, Herbert Barry III, Irvin L. Child

Drinking in Different Cultures, Nov 1956, Herbert Barry III, Margaret K. Bacon

Temporal Factors in Visual Discrimination, May 1956, Herbert Barry III, Irvin L. Child

www.ingramcontent.com/pod-product-compliance
Lightning Source LLC
Chambersburg PA
CBHW041616120626
46551CB00003B/461